THE OPEN DOOR

THE OPEN DOOR

ONE HUNDRED POEMS, ONE HUNDRED YEARS OF *POETRY* MAGAZINE

Edited by Don Share and
Christian Wiman

THE UNIVERSITY OF CHICAGO PRESS

Chicago and London

The University of Chicago Press, Chicago 60637
The University of Chicago Press, Ltd., London
© 2012 by The Poetry Foundation
All rights reserved. Published 2012.
Paperback edition 2013
Printed in the United States of America

22 21 20 19 18 17 16 15 14 13   6 7 8 9

ISBN-13: 978-0-226-75070-5 (cloth)
ISBN-13: 978-0-226-10401-0 (paperback)
ISBN-13: 978-0-226-75073-6 (e-book)
DOI: 10.7208/chicago/9780226750736.001.0001

Library of Congress Cataloging-in-Publication Data

The open door : one hundred poems, one hundred years of Poetry magazine /
edited by Don Share and Christian Wiman.
        pages.   cm.
ISBN-13: 978-0-226-75070-5 (cloth : alkaline paper)
ISBN-13: 978-0-226-75073-6 (e-book)
ISBN-10: 0-226-75070-1 (cloth : alkaline paper)
ISBN-10: 0-226-75073-6 (e-book) 1. American poetry. I. Share, Don 1957–
II. Wiman, Christian, 1966–   III. Poetry (Chicago, Ill.)
PS613.O64 2012
811'.508—dc23

2011053099

♾ This paper meets the requirements of
ANSI/NISO Z39.48-1992 (Permanence of Paper).

Contents

Mastery and Mystery:
Twenty-One Ways to Read a Century
1

Editors' Note
19

Mastery and Mystery

Twenty-One Ways to Read a Century

CHRISTIAN WIMAN

One way to think of Modernism in poetry is of fragments anxious about their origins. "These fragments I have shored against my ruins," wrote T. S. Eliot in (and of) *The Waste Land* in 1922. "I cannot make it cohere," wrote Ezra Pound some fifty years later, at the end of his epic avalanche of allusions and music and madness, *The Cantos.* Poetry has changed a lot in the last hundred years, but it still lives with and within this tension. The best of it draws equal strength from both poles: the power of the fragment depends upon the pull of its original context; but also, the credibility of the unity that any part implies depends upon the integrity and lonely singularity of that part. There is some combination of mastery and mystery: language has been honed to unprecedented degrees of precision, but it exists within—and in some way acknowledges—some primal and nearly annihilating silence. "The beast that lives on silence," as W. S. Graham put it, "takes / Its bite out of either side":

I'll give the beast a quick skelp
And through Art you'll hear it yelp.

. . .

Mastery and mystery: add a hundred years and you have an incredibly vital and seemingly unkillable movement, for Modernism remains stubbornly, strikingly persistent even in the work of those poets who react against it. It might be too much to argue that W S.

Di Piero's 2004 poem "Big City Speech" (139)[1] wouldn't even exist without Ezra Pound's "In a Station of the Metro" (21), which appeared in *Poetry* ninety-one years earlier. But still, the radiant discreteness of Di Piero's observations, the way they seem to float in some uncontainable space, the weird piercing clarity whose meaning is only (only!) its own electric existence and the real world that sparks alive within it: listen closely, and you can hear a whole century echoing:

> your gorgeous color-chart container ships
> and cab-top numbers squinting in the mist

Or, less obviously, take Don Paterson's "The Lie" (146). With its regular rhymes, its careful but comfortably familiar meter, its form could fit easily in the nineteenth century, at least until the bomb of its subject—a child locked in a basement, a lie trapped in a mind—explodes. Part of the horror of this poem is its vertiginous inwardness, the way it feels ripped out of some original and unrecoverable reality. In this case the source is psychological and not historical, but the same Modernist dynamic of a present reality underpinned and undermined by its missing source is at play.

. . .

Mastery and mystery: add an intrepid woman, Harriet Monroe, who wanted a magazine equal to the art and architecture she saw everywhere around her in turn-of-the-century Chicago; add ninety years of persistence and poverty, a dozen editors feeding and herding poets like feral cats; add a $200 million windfall in 2002 from the reclusive Ruth Lilly, and you have a seemingly unkillable magazine. (I wanted to steal a line from Charles Bukowski (85) and call this book *The Stupidity of Our Endurance*, but not everyone shared my suicidal sense of irony.) As A. R. Ammons once wrote: "The histories of modern poetry in America and of *Poetry* in America are almost interchangeable, certainly inseparable."

. . .

Almost. What an abyss of arguments and temperaments, masterpieces and missed opportunities, taste and the lack thereof opens up in that

---

1. Text references are to this volume.

word. Pretty much every post-Modernist poet of significance has published in *Poetry*, but not every poet has published his or her best poems there, and Don Share and I decided early on that in this book we would focus on poems, not names, that we would celebrate poetry, not *Poetry*. Thus we have approached the archive just as we do the hundred thousand submissions that come into our offices each year, poem by poem, with an eye out for the unexpected—the one-off masterpiece that juts up like a mountain from the landscape you thought you knew (see Belle Randall's "A Child's Garden of Gods" on page 169), the bizarre rhetorical shriek that history and fury seem to have conspired to create (see George Starbuck's "Of Late" on page 76), the little-known gem by the much-anthologized master (see Wallace Stevens's "Tea at the Palaz of Hoon" on page 63). We have also aimed, as we always do, at an audience that is not comprised entirely of specialists, with Harriet Monroe's first editorial firmly in mind:

> We believe that there is a public for poetry, that it will grow, and that as it becomes more numerous and appreciative the work produced in this art will grow in power, in beauty, in significance.

. . .

A public for poetry. Now there's a notion that's been kicked around for a hundred years, especially the last twenty or so. I've contributed to this myself at times—rather ignominiously, it now seems to me. The discussions always begin with the assumption that, because poetry is not present in the culture in the way that, say, movies are, or even some literary fiction that captures the country's attention for a while, then poetry has no meaning for that culture, no effect on it. Never mind the fact that this is demonstrably untrue by some practical measurements—the circulation of *Poetry* is much higher than it's ever been, the Poetry Foundation's website has two million unique blah blah—that's not really the point. Whenever I hear this negative sentiment now, I think of the argument that roiled American politics several years ago about whether we—America, I mean—should drill for oil in the Arctic National Wildlife Refuge. Why not? We need the oil. The place being considered was so remote that it might as well have been on the moon. And as for being the breeding ground of the porcupine caribou, what the hell is a porcupine caribou? Drill, baby, drill.

The strongest argument against this action was never, to my knowledge, spoken, perhaps because it's seemingly the weakest. It's also completely apolitical. You don't need to know a thing about quantum entanglement, wherein one atom can affect another even though they are separated by tremendous distance, to have some sense that our lives are always larger than the physical limitations within which they occur. We exist apart from our existences, you might say; we are connected to the world and to other people in ways we will never be able to fully articulate or understand—and we assert our iron wills and ravenous hungers at our own peril. There is such a thing as a collective unconscious. There is such a thing as a spirit of place, and it reaches beyond geography. And poetry, which is a kind of quantum entanglement in language, is not simply a way of helping us to recognize the relations we have with people and places but a means of preserving and protecting those relations. For many people, true, poetry will remain remote, inaccessible, and on the same plane of perception as that Arctic refuge. But who knows by what unconscious routes poetry is reaching into lives that seem to have nothing to do with it? Who knows what atomic energies are unleashed by a solitary man or woman quietly encountering some arrangement of language that gives their being—shunted aside by chores and fears and who knows what—back to them? This is why I regret adding to the clamor over poetry's "relevance." The reaction is defensive and misguided, not because there is no hope for elevating poetry's importance but because its power is already greater than any public attention can confer upon it.

. . .

In the American public imagination, though, poetry has a hothouse tinge to it. It's tweedy, and tweet-y, and has little to do with the bill-paying, stock-checking, dirty-diaper lives lived by most people. Poets themselves have been partly responsible for this. We have argued over esoteric or territorial issues that no one outside of the poetry world could possibly care about. We have embalmed poems in sociology, have created a kind of machine-speak critical jargon that any sane person would simply laugh at. We have exalted poets whose verbal and associative skills are immense but who have, finally, not very much to say. H. G. Wells once famously described Henry James as a hippopotamus trying to pick up a pea. He meant it to be the severest of insults, but *at least there was a pea.*

The tide is changing on all of this. Just glance at some of the more recent contributors to this volume and you'll see that poets are recognizing and reclaiming the primal power of the art they practice—and not simply on an abstract or spiritual level either. Have a look at Jacob Saenz's poem (161) about the rounding up of illegal immigrants back in 2007. At the time, newspapers were filled with accounts of the event. How many times have you thought of it since? What has happened to those people? Pound said, famously, that poetry is news that stays news. Thousands of people will come across this little poem now, with its deceptive lilt and tricky music, its playful way of leading us right into blindnesses we would rather not face, its skewering conclusion that connects huge and seemingly unstoppable events with decisions we all make in our daily lives; thousands of people will read this poem and it will be—if they are going to *be*—a thorn in their brains. Or have a look at Thomas Sayers Ellis's "Or" (102), which hones in on one sound—a soft sound, paradoxically—through all sorts of playful and awful permutations, until it seems to become a sort of fist pounding the podium before an impenetrable audience. You're the audience. And that silence ramifying around Ellis's last line? That's your life.

· · ·

Why are these poems so intricately wrought, so far from "normal" speech? Because, as Pound also said, "technique is the test of a man's sincerity." Formal decisions are ethical decisions. The sound and form of the poem are everything; they buffet it against its hard journey through time and indifference. Or, to change the metaphor, they enable it to insinuate itself into the hard carapace of our consciousness, so that the poem's "message"—*Look up from your insulated life*, in these instances, *Enlarge your idea of what it means to be human*—won't just bounce off the glaze of us. Craft matters because life matters. Craftless poetry is not only as perishable as the daily paper, it's meretricious, disrespectful (of its subjects as well as its readers), and sometimes, as Pound implies, even unethical.

· · ·

The difficulty of modern poetry—that is, poetry written since Modernism—is taken by most people as a given. One need only glance at poems like Edna St. Vincent Millay's "Rendezvous" (93), William Matthews's "Mingus at the Showplace" (53), or any number of other poems in this book to reveal the fallacy of that assumption. But never mind: it *is* true that some of the poetry written during the past hundred years or so makes some extreme demands of readers. *Briggflatts* (64), by Basil Bunting, which appeared in its entirety in *Poetry* in 1966 and which now seems obviously one of the greatest poems of the twentieth century, is sometimes taken as an exemplar of this difficulty. If you are not very familiar with poetry, you will likely have some trouble figuring out exactly what is being described, which is fine, which is, in fact, exactly what the poet intended. Besides being "about" a man who realizes, way too late, that the most intense and defining experience of his life occurred during an adolescent love affair, *Briggflatts* is a palimpsest of history, nature, learning, loss. It is the testament and artifact of a man who has lived so thoroughly into the language, so thoroughly *through* the language, that it has become a purely expressive medium. Because of cadence and pacing, and the way sounds echo and intensify sense, the word is restored to a kind of primal relation with the world; language itself takes on the textures and heft of things:

Under sacks on the stone
two children lie,
hear the horse stale,
the mason whistle,
harness mutter to shaft,
felloe to axle squeak,
rut thud the rim,
crushed grit.

. . .

As a general rule, it's safe to say that if you can paraphrase a poem, it's not a poem. There's no other way of saying what Bunting is saying in *Briggflatts*. The language is *action*. Great poetry is usually difficult in some way, and then clear in ways we would never expect. ("It is easier to die than to remember"—Bunting) Its difficulty, you might say, makes new clarities possible in and for us. "I wanted to write a poem / that you would understand," wrote William Carlos Williams,

> for what good is it to me
> if you can't understand it?
>   —But you got to try hard.

· · ·

Part of the enjoyment of poetry—an enormous part—is letting yourself experience things you do not understand, letting the textures and rhythms of verse take you to places in your consciousness—and unconciousness—that you could not have accessed otherwise. E. E. Cummings's "What If a Much of a Which of a Wind" is an obvious example: to have its rare near-clarities mean anything ("all nothing's only our hugest home") you have to let yourself be blown around in the word-wind for a while. But the example needn't be so conspicuous: Denise Levertov's "Our Bodies" (134) is a little master class in free verse, and if you don't read it the way its line breaks dictate—don't *feel* its form happening viscerally in you—then its effect is not simply diminished but actually distorted. Take the opening three lines:

> Our bodies, still young under
> the engraved anxiety of our
> faces . . .

The mind naturally wants to read these lines like this:

> Our bodies, still young
> under the engraved anxiety
> of our faces . . .

But this completely changes the meaning and effect of the lines. It is one thing to say that a body is "still young," quite another to say that it is "still young under." The latter implies a history, a density of feeling and experience, whereas the former is simply a statement of fact. Similarly, the awkward pause at the end of the second line intensifies the sensation of anxiety being described, and that word "our" that's stranded unnaturally there for a moment enhances one's feeling for, and sensation of, the precarious marriage of loneliness and communion that marks any authentic love.

The point here is not to go through every poem nitpicking technique, trying to find some obvious "reason" for every formal decision. Rather, the point is simply to be aware that what may seem like awkwardness or even randomness in poetry (James Schuyler!) can be as formally severe and singular as any Bach fugue.

.   .   .

Most poets I know read almost unconsciously at first, feeling the poem's formal and linguistic dynamics as much as its "meaning" (in the end, there is no way to separate meaning from a poem's form and sound). Meaning matters, of course, and most poems do have some bedrock denotative sense upon which the mind can rest (all of the poems in this book do). But still, some mystery usually remains. Poetry, like life, has its patches of pure black, its furthest interiors where meaning gleams darkly, and must remain in that darkness if it is to mean at all. You know a good poem by whether or not those irreducible dark spots are integral to your experience of the whole. "Our only obscurities should be those we are driven into," the almost-forgotten English poet Ruth Pitter once wrote, "then a sort of blessing may descend, making such obscurity magical."

.   .   .

"Reading in silence is the source of half the misconceptions that have caused the public to distrust poetry." That's Bunting again. It's a statement worth keeping in mind when reading every single poem in this book.

.   .   .

One of the qualities essential to being good at reading poetry is also one of the qualities essential to being good at life: a capacity for surprise. It's easy to become so mired in our likes or dislikes that we can no longer recall that person who once responded to poems—and to people—without any preconceived notions of what we wanted them to be. The irony is that one of poetry's powers is to reanimate a reality that has gone gray for us, or maybe not gray, maybe perfectly pleasant but ungraspable somehow, the days flashing past like images seen from a train. Time seems to accelerate as we get older because the brain becomes habituated to its circumstances and surroundings—the bills, the commutes, the kiss on the cheek goodnight—and part of the brain shuts down. Then you look up, and a decade seems to have slipped right through your fingers. "And yet the ways we miss our lives," wrote Randall Jarrell, "are life."

Poetry cuts right into this glaze (like that line from Jarrell, for instance) in two ways. First, it simply gives us access to a new world and new experience (you might have been familiar with Northumbrian gravestone making before Bunting, but I wasn't); and second, and more crucially, it enlivens the lives we thought we knew, it slows them down, or gives us eyes more capable of perceiving their passing. It makes us see the latent strangeness within—and feel our dormant spirits beneath—numb habit.

Consider Craig Arnold, a forty-two-year-old poet who vanished three years ago while hiking a remote volcano in Japan. As fate would have it, Don and I read his poem "Meditation on a Grapefruit" (57) the very day that he disappeared, and the poem so shocked us out of our own mental insulation that we immediately sent off the acceptance e-mail that Craig would never see. Such a tiny thing, "To come to the kitchen / and peel a little basketball / for breakfast" on a day like any other; to feel and smell "a cloud of oil / misting out of its pinprick pores / clean and sharp as pepper"; to adhere to this "discipline" that is "precisely pointless":

a pause   a little emptiness

each year harder to live within
each year harder to live without

.   .   .

Why write poetry? I don't mean just the "professional" poet (there is no such thing), the poet whose life is ineluctably bound up with, and confusingly shunted aside by, words—but also the undergraduate who finds herself spending more time on her creative writing assignments than anything else, the judge who scrawls a quatrain on the back of an envelope, the housewife who keeps a journal that she'd burn before showing to anyone. Why is this obsession so widespread in our culture, and why is it found in every culture we know?

Lisel Mueller has one answer, in a poem that appeared in *Poetry* in 1987. Stunned by the death of her mother, the speaker of this poem—an adolescent, presumably, though the age is not specified—wanders out to the "lovingly planted garden" where the "day lilies were as deaf / as the ears of drunken sleepers / and the roses curved inward." Here is how the poem ends:

> I sat on a gray stone bench
> ringed with the ingénue faces
> of pink and white impatiens
> and placed my grief
> in the mouth of language,
> the only thing that would grieve with me.

Implicit in that last line is an assumption that language is a living thing, with a kind of consciousness, that it returns or reciprocates the attention that is turned toward it. Not just any attention, though, but only our fullest and most costly consciousness, only our whole selves honed by emotional extremity. Language has no life unless and until we give it ours:

> Now in one year
>   a book published
>   and plumbing—
> took a lifetime
>   to weep
>   a deep
>   trickle,
>
> (Lorine Niedecker)

·   ·   ·

"The poetic gift won't tolerate vanity," writes Nadezhda Mandelstam. This might come as a surprise to anyone who has suffered through supper with some bloviating laureate, or even endured an ordinary open-mike night at any local bar. It's important to point out, then, that what Mandelstam means has little to do with the poet as a public presence and everything to do with the solitary self that blindly senses its way toward—and very rarely joltingly suffers—

his gift. Many poets go out into the world like cock-eyed roosters (the masculine symbol is not accidental; women seem, in my experience, better at managing this dynamic) precisely because they feel the negligible control they have over the very thing for which they are praised; it is a compensatory gesture, and a protective one. And what is true of the consciousness of the artist, that it must be vulnerable, must remain open to a power that it can never own—"Think assailable thoughts," writes Jane Hirshfield, "or be lonely"—is true of the work of art. It must be assailable in some sense. When Wallace Stevens argues against Christianity in his most famous poem "Sunday Morning," which appeared in *Poetry* in November 1915; when he says that "Death is the mother of beauty" and Christianity is a flinch away from the beauty and integrity of a fully lived life, it is crucial to the effect of the poem that he makes his argument in grand Biblical cadences that recall—and even confusingly reawaken—all the splendor of what he is ostensibly renouncing. Similarly, in "Tea at the Palaz of Hoon" (63), which seems to be a straightforward celebration of the absolute power and self-sufficiency of the individual imagination, simply the fact that Stevens includes a "you" to dispute that assertion, and that the "you" sees the speaker's self-sufficiency as utter loneliness, haunts—and paradoxically intensifies—the effect of his final claim: "And there I found myself more truly and more strange."

. . .

Religion often seems a bit crude when thinking of poems—a dimming of energy, part of the critical intelligence, an encrustation. There is an animus, an élan vital, a force that moves through verse at the speed of god. To assert this—to assent to it—is not idolatry but humility. Religion is human; it's what one *does* with intense spiritual experience; it's necessary (for some) but secondary. There is in poetry a power, a presence, coextensive with our earliest instincts, including those that drove us to create religions. That's why even poems that seem to renounce religion can mysteriously restore one's feeling for it, because without that original charge of heart and blood, without that first marriage of word and world, all that has emerged subsequently is merely intellectual, and lifeless. Most "devotional" poetry of the past hundred years is aimed at this ur-impulse, at sparking it back to life:

in words of need and hope striving
to awaken the old keeper of the living
and restore lasting melodies of his desire.

(Robert Duncan)

This focus, I think, this primary fidelity, is why even the poems that deal with spiritual matters directly tend to avoid specific religions. T. S. Eliot's late work is a marked exception, and powerful for being so. So is Mary Karr's "Disgraceland" (44), though her fast-talking confession and apparently flippant (it isn't, really) tone reveal her uneasiness and ambivalence about assenting to the structure of given religion. Note how the scattershot proliferation of images, which mirror the speaker's lifelong confusion, gain focus near the end of this poem. Even the language slows down—"some jade wave buoyed me forward"—as if the whole poem were concentrating on what came next. This, too, is the province of poetry, to reattach rituals to their sources, to make us feel the radical strangeness of actions we may have come to take for granted:

> and I found myself upright
>   in the instant, with a garden
>   inside my own ribs aflourish.
>
> There, the arbor leafs.
>   The vines push out plump grapes.
>   You are loved, someone said. Take that
>
>   and eat it.

.   .   .

For the past century the emphasis in American poetry has been on the lyric, and when we talk about lyric poetry we tend to think of emotional inwardness, even when the details of a given poem may be completely external. James Wright's "The Blessing" (137) is a classic example: the details of the natural world are rendered with a kind of inner spiritual precision that enables the poet almost, but not quite, to transcend them:

Suddenly I realize
That if I stepped out of my body I would break
Into blossom.

But the lyric, as this anthology clearly reveals, is not limited to in-
ward experience. Thom Gunn's "Lines for a Book" (173) is a lyric
poem, but there is no sense of inwardness at all, no mystery emanat-
ing off of it. Gunn had little patience with anything that smacked
of Romantic effluvia. As it happens, I lived around the corner from
him for a time in San Francisco. With his heroic height and Spartan
crewcut, his motorcycle boots and black leather jacket, he would
have been menacing had he not been so disconcertingly courte-
ous—the impeccable English accent helped—and kind. But still,
Gunn savored places most of us would fear to enter, and when he
wrote about "toughs," as he did frequently, he did so with the au-
thority that comes from direct experience. "It's better," he wrote,

To be insensitive, to steel the will,
Than sit irresolute all day at stool
Inside the heart . . .

I don't know who Gunn was referring to here, but it might have
been the great German Modernist Rainer Maria Rilke ("Everything
is disappearing inward") or, more likely, the many American imita-
tors who tamed his terrible Angels with teabag mysticism and pre-
dictable epiphanies. (To experienced readers, the end of "The Bless-
ing" may seem a familiar move by this point, but it was shocking and
radical when it was written—and the poem, for all its soft spots, re-
tains an eerie, affecting power.) Gunn wanted to obliterate personal-
ity in his poetry; his great models were the poets of the English Re-
naissance. It was a directly opposite tack to that of the Confessional
poets, whose perceptions had everything to do with the personali-
ties from which they emanated. Sylvia Plath is thought of as one of
the first Confessional poets, but this is not really accurate. With her
extreme staginess, the blurred sense of self and speaker, the carefully
projected hysteria, her work, in terms of how much personality is in
play, actually has more in common with Gunn's than with the Con-
fessional poets she is thought to have spawned. James Wright's "The

Blessing," on the other hand, for all of its apparent focus outward, is a poem in which you can not only feel a distinct personality (tenderhearted, mystically inclined) but also its absolute necessity to the effect of the poem. Others in this book include the William Matthews and Mary Karr poems I've already mentioned. The speakers of these latter poems are like lively, idiosyncratic, first-person narrators of good novels—with all the rewards and limitations thereof.

. . .

A writer who grows up in a bookless culture—"the folk from whom all poetry flows," as Lorine Niedecker put it, "and dreadfully much else"—will always be torn by conflicting impulses. On one hand, the Culture she acquires—she will always think of it with a capital C—separates her from the culture in which she was raised. On the other hand, everything in her that might animate her intellectual acquisitions is rooted in the world she has left. The novelist and poet (and frequent *Poetry* contributor) Reynolds Price once spoke of the terrible risk a writer takes by uprooting herself from her native place. But it's also a risk *not* to leave, since it sometimes requires distance to clearly see the place—James Joyce's Ireland, say—in which one came to consciousness.

This book begins with a famous little poem by the consummate Modernist Ezra Pound, who left Hailey, Idaho (it was still the Idaho Territory, actually) at the age of eighteen and spent his life acquiring world culture with an assiduity that was as impressive as it was impossible, like a python trying to swallow a camel. The anthology ends with a late poem of W. B. Yeats, who certainly didn't grow up in a bookless culture (his father was a famous painter) but nonetheless felt the tension between his literary aspirations and his geographical inspirations. Though he was a fixture in literary London for decades, and though his international voice and acclaim eventually brought him a Nobel Prize, Yeats remained staunchly connected and committed to Ireland, even if that Ireland was in part a dream. "The Fisherman" (183), one of the most beautiful poems Yeats ever wrote, captures all the simplicity and complexity of this relation:

> Maybe a twelve-month since
> Suddenly I began,

In scorn of this audience,
Imagining a man,
And his sun-freckled face
And gray Connemara cloth,
Climbing up to a place
Where stone is dark with froth,
And the down turn of his wrist
When the flies drop in the stream—
A man who does not exist,
A man who is but a dream;
And cried, "Before I am old
I shall have written him one
Poem maybe as cold
And passionate as the dawn."

Every poem in this book is situated somewhere on this spectrum between life and learning, between linguistic powers honed to surgical precisions and the messy living reality out of which all language, if it would stay alive, must be rooted.

. . .

For if it is true that the closer bound the artist is to his community the harder it is for him to see with a detached vision, it is also true that when he is too isolated, though he may see clearly enough what he does see, that dwindles in quantity and importance.

This authoritative quote from W. H. Auden is illuminating, useful, and wrong. It expresses (more succinctly) some of what I've said above, but it hasn't (and how could it?) taken into account what the word "community" might mean and how our notions of that would change over the years. Adrian Blevins might not speak for a community bound by highways and mores, but the one she does speak for in "How to Cook a Wolf" (155)—"the dumbstruck story of the American female"—is considerably larger. Rae Armantrout—whose entire work, by the way, might be read as an acerbic reaction to, or defiant expansion of, lyric poetry—also addresses or mirrors our worries of community, in this life and the next, and with a dash of weird and welcome humor that might make you underestimate her seriousness:

Hectic and flexible

flames

are ideal

new bodies for us!

.   .   .

For all the canons and anthologies, for every rock-solid reputation and critical consensus, poetry is personal or it is nothing. That is, until a poem has been tested on your own pulse, to paraphrase John Keats, until you have made up your own mind and heart about where you stand in relation to it, and it to you—until this happens, all poetry is merely literature, all reading rote. It's true that some people are better readers of poetry than others; that some people's judgments matter (for the culture as a whole) more than others; that, just as with music or art, there are elements of craft and historical perspective essential to being *able* to formulate a meaningful response. But still, poetry is made up of poems, and poems repulse and entice in unpredictable ways, and anyone who reads independently and spiritedly is going to carry an eccentric canon around in his head. This is half the fun of it all.

.   .   .

Reading through a hundred years of *Poetry*, week after week of issue after issue, some forty thousand poems in all, Don and I, when we weren't rendered prone and moaning, jolted back and forth between elation and depression. Here's a hundred pages of work by a Pulitzer Prize winner, whose poems, just a couple of decades after his death, feel ambered in a dead idiom. Here's two hundred pages of poems that stirred contemporaries to comparisons of Shakespeare, without one moment now that seems fresh, necessary, worth saving. Here's poet after poet whose names you've never even heard, some with lines that leap up out of poems like the limb of a prodded lab frog, then flop back down in the cold poems to which they are ineluctably bound. On the other hand, here's Josephine Miles, whose work I'd never even paused over, and the irascible, irrepressible Paul Goodman (out, but just barely), and James Laughlin with his wonderful winking ambition to be nothing more than a foot-note, perhaps in "the *Obloquies* of / Dreadful Edward Dahlberg." Or Dahlberg! How badly we wanted to include his weird prose piece titled—aggressively, no doubt—"Five Poems." "My friendship with Dahlberg," Fanny Howe wrote in *Poetry* half a century later, after giving a heartbreaking sense of the man's volatile intensity and prophetic authority, his absolute seriousness of purpose, "ended bit-terly. He chased me around his apartment on Rivington Street with his pants down." And that's how it is, this life in poetry, the pathos mixed right in with the bathos, the heroic sense of purpose with the pathetic pull of circumstance. "What do you do?" asks the man on the airplane, and for a moment every American poet pauses as one, feeling that face-off between spiritual integrity and social insecurity. And that's sort of what we feel too, Don and I, after being buried under a hundred years of poems. Humility, first: to think of all the lives behind this work, and the element of chance that has made us, for a moment, the judges of it. And pride: to be a part of it, to have our own lives so richly entangled.

Editors' Note

All of the quotations included in this anthology come from either the "Comment" section of *Poetry*, which comprises the back half of the magazine each month, or from the lively letters that have passed between poets and the editors of *Poetry* over the years. These quotations are not meant to be representative, nor do the selections indicate our perception of the "best" prose writers throughout the magazine's history. Our foremost criterion for inclusion was that the quotes be at once memorable and completely self-contained, and some of the best writing in the magazine does not always have these isolated, detachable instants. The quotes are also not intended to separate the poems into thematic sections, though they are placed in ways that we hope will both clarify and inspire readers' responses to the nearby poems.

Except for a couple of instances when living authors or heirs have insisted on using the latest versions of poems, all of the poems in this anthology conform to their original appearance in *Poetry*.

The Open Door will be the policy of this magazine—
may the great poet we are looking for never find it
shut, or half-shut, against his ample genius! To this end
the editors hope to keep free of entangling alliances
with any single class or school. They desire to print
the best English verse which is being written today,
regardless of where, by whom, or under what theory
of art it is written.

HARRIET MONROE, 1912

EZRA POUND

In a Station of the Metro

The apparition   of these faces   in the crowd   :
Petals   on a wet, black   bough   .

April 1913

KAY RYAN

Sharks' Teeth

Everything contains some
silence. Noise gets
its zest from the
small shark's-tooth
shaped fragments
of rest angled
in it. An hour
of city holds maybe
a minute of these
remnants of a time
when silence reigned,
compact and dangerous
as a shark. Sometimes
a bit of a tail
or fin can still
be sensed in parks.

April 2004

MARIE PONSOT

Anti-Romantic

I explain ontology, mathematics, theophily,
Symbolic and Aristotelian logic, says the tree.

I demonstrate perspective's and proportion's ways.
I elucidate even greyness by my greys and greys and greys.

Gravity's laws, the four dimensions, Sapphic imagery,
Come from contemplating me,
Says the tree.

I perfectly exhibit the functions of earth and air:
Look up, at and through, my branches, leaved, budded, or bare
Laid in their luminous degrees against lustrous infinity:
Your seeing relates you to all of space, through me.
Here's aesthetics, too. No sight's nearer to perfectly fair.
I am mediate and immediate, says the tree.

I am variable, exquisite, tough,
Even useful; I am subtle; all this is enough.
I don't want to be a temple, says the tree.
But if you don't behave, I will be.

March 1958

The Young

You bastards! It's all sherbet, and folly
makes you laugh like mules. Chances
dance off your wrists, each day ready,

sprites in your bones and spite not yet
swollen, not yet set. You gather handful
after miracle handful, seeing straight,

reaching the lighthouse in record time,
pockets brim with scimitar things. Now
is not a pinpoint but a sprawling realm.

Bewilderment and thrill are whip-quick
twins, carried on your backs, each vow
new to touch and each mistake a broken

biscuit. I was you. Sea robber boarding
the won galleon. Roaring trees. Machines
without levers, easy in bowel and lung.

One cartwheel over the quicksand curve
of Tuesday to Tuesday and you're gone,
summering, a ship on the farthest wave.

December 2008

LEROI JONES

Valéry as Dictator

Sad. And it comes
tomorrow. Again, grey, the streaks
of work
shedding the stone
of the pavement, dissolving
with the idea
of singular endeavour. Herds, the
herds
of suffering intelligences
bunched,
and out of
hearing. Though the day
come to us
      in waves,
           sun, air, the beat
of the clock.
        Though I stare at the radical
world,
     wishing it would stand still.
              Tell me,
and I gain at the telling.
Of the lie, and the waking
against the heavy breathing
of new light, dawn, shattering
the naive cluck
of feeling.
       What is tomorrow
that it cannot come
         today?

December 1963

Note: LeRoi Jones changed his name to Amiri Baraka in 1967.

Don't be "viewy"—leave that to the writers of pretty little philosophic essays. Don't be descriptive; remember that the painter can describe a landscape much better than you can, and that he has to know a deal more about it.

EZRA POUND, March 1913

I would trade the bulk of contemporary anecdotal free verse for more incisive, chilling poetry. . . . There's more pathos in a poetry that recognizes the universe is central; the poor human, eccentric.

ANGE MLINKO, October 2007

Eros Turannos

She fears him, and will always ask
   What fated her to choose him;
She meets in his engaging mask
   All reasons to refuse him;
But what she meets and what she fears
Are less than are the downward years,
Drawn slowly to the foamless weirs
   Of age, were she to lose him.

Between a blurred sagacity
   That once had power to sound him,
And Love, that will not let him be
   The seeker that she found him,
Her pride assuages her, almost,
As if it were alone the cost.
He sees that he will not be lost,
   And waits, and looks around him.

A sense of ocean and old trees
   Envelops and allures him;
Tradition, touching all he sees
   Beguiles and reassures him;
And all her doubts of what he says
Are dimmed with what she knows of days,
Till even prejudice delays,
   And fades—and she secures him.

The falling leaf inaugurates
   The reign of her confusion;
The pounding wave reverberates
   The crash of her illusion;
And home, where passion lived and died,
Becomes a place where she can hide,—
While all the town and harbor side
   Vibrate with her seclusion.

We tell you, tapping on our brows,
   The story as it should be,—
As if the story of a house
   Were told, or ever could be;
We'll have no kindly veil between
Her visions and those we have seen,—
As if we guessed what hers have been
   Or what they are, or would be.

Meanwhile, we do no harm; for they
   That with a god have striven,
Not hearing much of what we say,
   Take what the god has given;
Though like waves breaking it may be,
Or like a changed familiar tree,
Or like a stairway to the sea,
   Where down the blind are driven.

March 1914

ANGE MLINKO

It Was a Bichon Frisé's Life . . .

Louisiana skies paddle north nodding hello to some exiles
displaced by floodwaters so we all putter in the bisque
in fretted dresses, alleviated by a fan. But we have nothing on

"Le Matin," in whose rococo frame a curtain sweeps to bare
a boudoir, a Bichon Frisé worrying something between paws,
begging the dulcet glance of the mistress whose push-up,

cupless corset and up-drawn stocking border what they
fall short of, per the stern frame rippling like a cloud!
Even the candle angles to get a look in the mirror

engloving the scene. Why it is her slipper the bitch clutches!
The gentleman's reverie is elsewhere . . . Loitering
Louisiana stops to admire this engraving by "N. Lavreinee."

What a chevalier! It makes the smeariest sunset think
it's in a Restoration Comedy, in such humidity
chefs defer meringues. "Ksar Rouge," "Taos Adobe,"

"Gulf Shrimp"—a thousand names of softboiled
lipsticks fritter English as if it were French, meaning
meeting no resistance from the flesh.

June 2008

MURIEL RUKEYSER

Song

The world is full of loss; bring, wind, my love,
    my home is where we make our meeting-place,
    and love whatever I shall touch and read
    within that face.

Lift, wind, my exile from my eyes;
    peace to look, life to listen and confess,
    freedom to find to find to find
    that nakedness.

October 1941

The Hereafter

At the gates to the Hereafter,
a rather drab affair, might as well be a union hall
in south Milwaukee, but with shackled
sweating bodies along the walls,
female, chiefly, and not at all miserable,
straining like bored sultanas at their fetters,
each of them singing a separate song.
A Semitic chap—the greeter, I suppose—
gives me the quick once-over
and most amused he seems to be. Has me figured.
Not unlike a gent I met only last week,
a salesman at a stereo shop on Broadway.
—*So*, he says. Nothing more.
—*Sew buttons*, says I, in a cavalier mood
and why not.
                    Ushers me into a tiny cinema,
a two-seater, really quite deluxe,
a great big Diet Coke in the cupholder,
fizzing away.
                    —*O.K.?* he asks.
I nod and the film unrolls.
A 20-million-dollar home movie it is,
featuring yours truly: at the foot
of the stairs with the dog, mounting
Josette in a new Smyrna love nest,
a fraught kitchen showdown with Mom,
the suicide, car wreck, home run.
You know what these things are like:
the outlandish hairdos, pastel bathroom fixtures.
The editing is out of this world,
the whole shebang in under an hour:
the air-raid drill on Wednesday morning,
1957, when Tito wet his pants;
there I am, beside myself with laughter,
miserable little creature.

The elemental, slow-motion machinery
of character's forcing house.
Even with all the fancy camera angles,
jump cuts and the rest,
might as well be a chain of short features:
Animal Husbandry, *Sexual Hygiene*,
Lisboa by Night . . .
What a lot of erections, voiding, pretzels,
bouncing the ball against the stoop.
She really did love you, all along.
These jealousies and rages of yours,
like a disgusting skin condition
that never goes away.
You, you . . .
What catalogs of failure, self-deception . . .
And then the lights come back on,
likewise the choir's splintered polyphony,
with its shards of *Sprechstimme*, the Ronettes, whatnot,
and in the air around us
something like the odor of a freshly spent cartridge,
when my minder asks brightly,

                              —*How about another Coke?*

                                 October 2003

The Love Song of J. Alfred Prufrock

S' io credessi che mia risposta fosse
A persona che mai tornasse al mondo,
Questa fiamma staria senza più scosse.
Ma perciocchè giammai di questo fondo
Non tornò vivo alcum, s' i' odo il vero,
Senza tema d' infamia ti rispondo.

Let us go then, you and I,
When the evening is spread out against the sky
Like a patient etherized upon a table;
Let us go, through certain half-deserted streets,
The muttering retreats
Of restless nights in one-night cheap hotels
And sawdust restaurants with oyster-shells:
Streets that follow like a tedious argument
Of insidious intent
To lead you to an overwhelming question . . .

Oh, do not ask, "What is it?"
Let us go and make our visit.

In the room the women come and go
Talking of Michelangelo.

The yellow fog that rubs its back upon the window panes,
The yellow smoke that rubs its muzzle on the window panes,
Licked its tongue into the corners of the evening,
Lingered upon the pools that stand in drains,
Let fall upon its back the soot that falls from chimneys,
Slipped by the terrace, made a sudden leap,
And seeing that it was a soft October night,
Curled once about the house, and fell asleep.

And indeed there will be time
For the yellow smoke that slides along the street,
Rubbing its back upon the window panes;
There will be time, there will be time
To prepare a face to meet the faces that you meet;
There will be time to murder and create,
And time for all the works and days of hands
That lift and drop a question on your plate:
Time for you and time for me,
And time yet for a hundred indecisions,
And for a hundred visions and revisions,
Before the taking of a toast and tea.

In the room the women come and go
Talking of Michelangelo.

And indeed there will be time
To wonder, "Do I dare?" and, "Do I dare?"—
Time to turn back and descend the stair,
With a bald spot in the middle of my hair—
(They will say: "How his hair is growing thin!")
My morning coat, my collar mounting firmly to the chin,
My necktie rich and modest, but asserted by a simple pin—
(They will say: "But how his arms and legs are thin!")
Do I dare
Disturb the universe?
In a minute there is time
For decisions and revisions which a minute will reverse.

For I have known them already, known them all:
Have known the evenings, mornings, afternoons,
I have measured out my life with coffee spoons;
I know the voices dying with a dying fall
Beneath the music from a farther room.
So how should I presume?

And I have known the eyes already, known them all—
The eyes that fix you in a formulated phrase.
And when I am formulated, sprawling on a pin,
When I am pinned and wriggling on the wall,
Then how should I begin
To spit out all the butt-ends of my days and ways?
     And how should I presume?

And I have known the arms already, known them all—
Arms that are braceleted and white and bare
(But in the lamplight, downed with light brown hair!)
    Is it perfume from a dress
    That makes me so digress?
Arms that lie along a table, or wrap about a shawl.
    And should I then presume?
     And how should I begin?

        . . .

Shall I say, I have gone at dusk through narrow streets,
And watched the smoke that rises from the pipes
Of lonely men in shirtsleeves, leaning out of windows? . . .

I should have been a pair of ragged claws
Scuttling across the floors of silent seas.

        . . .

And the afternoon, the evening, sleeps so peacefully!
Smoothed by long fingers,
Asleep . . . tired . . . or it malingers,
Stretched on the floor, here beside you and me.
Should I, after tea and cakes and ices,
Have the strength to force the moment to its crisis?
But though I have wept and fasted, wept and prayed,
Though I have seen my head (grown slightly bald) brought in
    upon a platter,
I am no prophet—and here's no great matter;
I have seen the moment of my greatness flicker,
And I have seen the eternal Footman hold my coat, and snicker,
    And in short, I was afraid.

And would it have been worth it, after all,
After the cups, the marmalade, the tea,
Among the porcelain, among some talk of you and me,
Would it have been worth while,
To have bitten off the matter with a smile,
To have squeezed the universe into a ball
To roll it towards some overwhelming question,
To say: "I am Lazarus, come from the dead,
Come back to tell you all, I shall tell you all"—
If one, settling a pillow by her head
      Should say: "That is not what I meant at all;
          That is not it, at all."

      And would it have been worth it, after all,
Would it have been worth while,
After the sunsets and the dooryards and the sprinkled streets,
After the novels, after the teacups, after the skirts that trail
      along the floor—
And this, and so much more?—
It is impossible to say just what I mean!
But as if a magic lantern threw the nerves in patterns on
      a screen:
Would it have been worth while
If one, settling a pillow or throwing off a shawl,
And turning toward the window, should say: "That is not it
      at all,
          That is not what I meant, at all."

                         .   .   .

      No! I am not Prince Hamlet, nor was meant to be;
Am an attendant lord, one that will do
To swell a progress, start a scene or two,
Advise the prince: withal, an easy tool,
Deferential, glad to be of use,
Politic, cautious, and meticulous;
Full of high sentence, but a bit obtuse;
At times, indeed, almost ridiculous—
Almost, at times, the Fool.

I grow old . . . I grow old . . .
I shall wear the bottoms of my trowsers rolled.

Shall I part my hair behind?   Do I dare to eat a peach?
I shall wear white flannel trowsers, and walk upon the beach.
I have heard the mermaids singing, each to each.
I do not think that they will sing to me.

I have seen them riding seaward on the waves,
Combing the white hair of the waves blown back
When the wind blows the water white and black.

We have lingered in the chambers of the sea
By seagirls wreathed with seaweed red and brown,
Till human voices wake us, and we drown.

.   .   .

June 1915

I do believe, desperately, in a "poetry of ideas." Poems have got, literally, to be about something. And the weights of love, murder, history, economics, etc., have got to drag whoever's writing in a personally sanctified direction or there will be no poems at all.

LEROI JONES (AMIRI BARAKA), March 1964

There has to be a little bit of muscle movement, it has to be alive in some sort of way. A moving poem doesn't just mean that it touches you, it means it has to move itself along as a going linguistic concern. Form is not like a pastry cutter—the dough has to move and discover its own shape.

SEAMUS HEANEY, December 2008

Look

Look! I bear into this room a platter piled high with the rage my mother felt toward my father! Yes, it's diamonds now. It's pearls, public humiliation, an angry dime-store clerk, a man passed out at the train station, a girl at the bookstore determined to read every fucking magazine on this shelf for free. They tell us that most of the billions of worlds beyond ours are simply desolate oceanless forfeits in space. But logic tells us there *must* be operas, there *have* to be car accidents cloaked in that fog. Down here, God just spit on a rock, and it became a geologist. God punched a hole in the drywall on earth and pulled out of that darkness another god. She—

just kept her thoughts to herself. She just—

followed him around the house, and every time he turned a light on, she turned it off.

October 2006

From "Eight Variations"

And when your beauty, washed away
In impure streams with my desire,
Is only topic for ill-mannered minds,
Gifted and glassy with exact recall,
Gossip and rancid footnotes, or remote despair,
Let ruined weather perish in the streets
And let the world's black lying flag come down.

Only in calendars that mark no Spring
Can there be weather in the mind
That moves to you again as you are now:
Tired after love and silent in this house,
Your back turned to me, quite alone,
Standing with one hand raised to smooth your hair,
At a small window, green with rain.

December 1942

ROBERT CREELEY

For Love

Yesterday I wanted to
speak of it, that sense above
the others to me
important because all

that I know derives
from what it teaches me.
Today, what is it that
is finally so helpless,

different, despairs of its own
statement, wants to
turn away, endlessly
to turn away.

If the moon did not . . .
no, if you did not
I wouldn't either, but
what would I not

do, what prevention, what
thing so quickly stopped.
That is love yesterday
or tomorrow, not

now. Can I eat
what you give me. I
have not earned it. Must
I think of everything

as earned. Now love also
becomes a reward so
remote from me I have
only made it with my mind.

Here is tedium,
despair, a painful
sense of isolation and
whimsical if pompous

self-regard. But that image
is only of the mind's
vague structure, vague to me
because it is my own.

Love, what do I think
to say. I cannot say it.
What have you become to ask,
what have I made you into,

companion, good company,
crossed legs with skirt, or
soft body under
the bones of the bed.

Nothing says anything
but that which it wishes
would come true, fears
what else might happen in

some other place, some
other time not this one.
A voice in my place, an
echo of that only in yours.

Let me stumble into
not the confession but
the obsession I begin with
now. For you

also (also)
some time beyond place, or
place beyond time, no
mind left to

say anything at all,
that face gone, now.
Into the company of love
it all returns.

May 1961 ·

Disgraceland

Before my first communion, I clung to doubt
    as Satan spider-like stalked
        the orb of dark surrounding Eden

for a wormhole into paradise.
    God had formed me from gel in my mother's womb,
        injected by my dad's smart shoot.

They swapped sighs until
    I came, smaller than a bite of burger.
        Quietly, I grew till my lungs were done

then the Lord sailed a soul
    like a lit arrow to inhabit me.
        Maybe that piercing

made me howl at birth,
    or the masked creatures whose scalpel
        cut a lightning bolt to free me.

I was hoisted by the heels and swatted, fed
    and hauled around. Time-lapse photos show
        my fingers grow past crayon outlines,

my feet come to fill spike heels.
    Eventually, I lurched out
        to kiss the wrong mouths, get stewed,

and sulk around. Christ always stood
    to one side with a glass of water.
        I swatted the sap away.

When my thirst got great enough to ask,
    a clear stream welled up inside,
        some jade wave buoyed me forward,

and I found myself upright
in the instant, with a garden
inside my own ribs aflourish.

There, the arbor leafs.
The vines push out plump grapes.
You are loved, someone said. Take that

and eat it.

January 2004

LUCILLE CLIFTON

sorrows

who would believe them winged
who would believe they could be

beautiful   who would believe
they could fall so in love with mortals

that they would attach themselves
as scars attach and ride the skin

sometimes we hear them in our dreams
rattling their skulls   clicking their bony fingers

envying our crackling hair
our spice filled flesh

they have heard me beseeching
as I whispered into my own

cupped hands   enough not me again
enough   but who can distinguish

one human voice
amid such choruses of desire

September 2007

Art is a thing of the individual. It is all very well to group by-gone artists into schools for class-room convenience. It amuses a certain type of mind to fasten tags upon living men. It interests readers and stimulates their curiosity to line artists up in opposing factions like the two sides of a base-ball game. But these are purely exterior phenomena and leave the profound individuality of the artist untouched.

AMY LOWELL, October 1914

I think poets should take the lesson of the great aromatic eucalyptus tree and poison the soil beneath us.

KAY RYAN, July 2005

On Visiting a Borrowed Country House in Arcadia

For John

To leave the city
Always takes a quarrel. Without warning,
Rancors that have gathered half the morning
Like things to pack, or a migraine, or a cloud,
Are suddenly allowed
To strike. They strike the same place twice.
We start by straining to be nice,
Then say something shitty.

Isn't it funny
How it's what *has* to happen
To make the unseen ivory gates swing open,
The rite we must perform so we can leave?
Always we must grieve
Our botched happiness: we goad
Each other till we pull to the hard shoulder of the road,
Yielding to tears inadequate as money.

But if instead
Of turning back, we drive into the day,
We forget the things we didn't say.
The silence fills with row on row
Of vines or olive trees. The radio
Hums to itself. We make our way between
Saronic blue and hills of glaucous green
And thread

Beyond the legend of the map
Through footnote towns along the coast
That boast
Ruins of no account—a column
More woebegone than solemn—
Men watching soccer at the two cafés
And half-built lots where dingy sheep still graze.
Climbing into the lap

Of the mountains now, we wind
Around blind, centrifugal turns.
The sun's great warship sinks and burns.
And where the roads without a sign are crossed,
We (inevitably) get lost.
Yet to be lost here
Still feels like being somewhere,
And we find

When we arrive and park,
No one minds that we are late—
There is no one to wait—
Only a bed to make, a suitcase to unpack.
The earth has turned her back
On one yellow middling star
To consider lights more various and far.
The shaggy mountains hulk into the dark

Or loom
Like slow, titanic waves. The cries
Of owls dilate the shadows. Weird harmonics rise
From the valley's distant glow, where coal
Extracted from the lignite mines must roll
On acres of conveyor belts that sing
The Pythagorean music of a string.
A huge grey plume

Of smoke or steam
Towers like the ghost of a monstrous flame
Or giant tree among the trees. And it is all the same—
The power plant, the forest, and the night,
The manmade light.
We are engulfed in an immense
Ancient indifference
That does not sleep or dream.

Call it Nature if you will,
Though everything that is is natural—
The lignite-bearing earth, the factory,
A darkness taller than the sky—
This out-of-doors that wins us our release
And temporary peace—
Not because it is pristine or pretty,
But because it has no pity or self-pity.

June 2007

CHARLES WRIGHT

Bedtime Story

The generator hums like a distant *ding an sich*.
It's early evening, and time, like the dog it is,
                         is hungry for food,
And will be fed, don't doubt it, will be fed, my small one.
The forest begins to gather its silences in.
The meadow regroups and hunkers down
                           for its cleft feet.

Something is wringing the rag of sunlight
                         inexorably out and hanging.
Something is making the reeds bend and cover their heads.
Something is licking the shadows up,
And stringing the blank spaces along, filling them in.
Something is inching its way into our hearts,
                 scratching its blue nails against the wall there.

Should we let it in?
                 Should we greet it as it deserves,
Hands on our ears, mouths open?
Or should we bring it a chair to sit on, and offer it meat?
Should we turn on the radio,
                 should we clap our hands and dance
The Something Dance, the welcoming Something Dance?
                 I think we should, love, I think we should.

                           March 2004

DELMORE SCHWARTZ

In the Naked Bed, In Plato's Cave

In the naked bed, in Plato's cave,
Reflected headlights slowly slid the wall,
Carpenters hammered beneath the shaded window,
Wind troubled the window curtains all night long.
A fleet of trucks strained uphill, grinding,
Their freights, as usual, hooded by tarpaulin.
The ceiling lightened again, the slanting diagram
Slid slowly off. Hearing the milkman's chop,
His striving up the stair, the bottle's chink,
I rose from bed, lit a cigarette,
And walked to the window. The stony street bestowed
The stillness in which buildings stand upon
The street-lamp's vigil, and the horse's patience.
The winter sky's pure capital
Turned me back to bed with exhausted eyes.

Strangeness grew in the motionless air. The loose
Film greyed. Shaking wagons, hooves' waterfalls
Sounded far off, increasing, louder and nearer.
A car coughed, starting up, Morning, softly
Melting the air, lifted the half-covered chair
From underseas, kindled the mirror
Upon the wall. The bird called tentatively, whistled,
Bubbled and whistled, so! Perplexed, still wet
With sleep, affectionate, hungry and cold. So, so,
O son of man, the ignorant night, the rumors
Of building and movement, the travail
Of early morning, the mystery of beginning
Again and again,
            while history is unforgiven.

January 1938

WILLIAM MATTHEWS

Mingus at the Showplace

I was miserable, of course, for I was seventeen,
and so I swung into action and wrote a poem,

and it was miserable, for that was how I thought
poetry worked: you digested experience and shat

literature. It was 1960 at The Showplace, long since
defunct, on West 4th St., and I sat at the bar,

casting beer money from a thin reel of ones,
the kid in the city, big ears like a puppy.

And I knew Mingus was a genius. I knew two
other things but they were wrong, as it happened.

So I made him look at the poem.
"There's a lot of that going around," he said,

and Sweet Baby Jesus he was right. He laughed
amiably. He didn't look as if he thought

bad poems were dangerous, the way some poets do.
If they were baseball executives they'd plot

to destroy sandlots everywhere so that the game
could be saved from children. Of course later

that night he fired his pianist in mid-number
and flurried him from the stand.

"We've suffered a diminuendo in personnel,"
he explained, and the band played on.

October 1991

DONALD JUSTICE

Men at Forty

Men at forty
Learn to close softly
The doors to rooms they will not be
Coming back to.

At rest on a stair-landing,
They feel it moving
Beneath them now like the deck of a ship,
Though the swell is gentle.

And deep in mirrors
They rediscover
The face of the boy as he practices tying
His father's tie there in secret,

And the face of that father,
Still warm with the mystery of lather.
They are more fathers than sons themselves now.
Something is filling them, something

That is like the twilight sound
Of the crickets, immense,
Filling the woods at the foot of the slope
Behind their mortgaged houses.

May 1966

To resist the reality of time is to resist leaving childhood behind. She called this resistance a flaw in herself, but is it? The self is not the soul, and it is the soul (coherence) that lives for nine years on earth in a potential state of liberty and harmony. Its openness to metamorphosis is usually sealed up during those early years until the self replaces the soul as the fist of survival.

FANNY HOWE, December 2008

Forecast

Isabel, I could vainly map a happy vale
Of dolls and balls and tell
The most various bears a really tale:
But lap to lap the fretting Isabel
Pale in her skinny pout, her wishing well
Is full of wishes no one can unspell.

Knots legs, knots arms, knots hair,
The world of tots smiles like a pumpkin
Into my despair,
I see the lightning in her summer stare,
And I would not by any bribe be kin
Or kith or share
In all the crying she will bring to bear.

May 1953

CRAIG ARNOLD

Meditation on a Grapefruit

To wake when all is possible
before the agitations of the day
have gripped you
        To come to the kitchen
and peel a little basketball
for breakfast
        To tear the husk
like cotton padding   a cloud of oil
misting out of its pinprick pores
clean and sharp as pepper
        To ease
each pale pink section out of its case
so carefully   without breaking
a single pearly cell
        To slide each piece
into a cold blue china bowl
the juice pooling   until the whole
fruit is divided from its skin
and only then to eat
        so sweet
          a discipline
precisely pointless   a devout
involvement of the hands and senses
a pause   a little emptiness

each year harder to live within
each year harder to live without

                 October 2009

The Hampton Institute Album

Down from another planet they have settled to mend
The bannisters. They wear bow ties and braces,
The flutings they polish with a polished hand.

Wingless, they build and repair
The mansions of what we have thought to be our inheritance.
Caution and candor they labor to maintain.

They are out of phase. I prepare
To burn all gentle structures, greek or thatch,
Under the masterful torch of my president here and abroad,

Till stubble outsmolders, and muslim and buddhist crack
In the orbit of kiln. A smoke
To some calm Christian planet will drift,

To where they are mending their mansions, beside whose doors
They are standing at ease, they are lifting the fans
Of unburdenable wings.

September 1967

Note: Hampton University (formerly the Hampton Institute) is a historically black university
located in Hampton, Virginia.

My Chosen Landscape

I am a continent, a violated geography,
Yet still I journey to this naked country
to seek a form which dances in the sand.
This is my chosen landscape.

GWENDOLYN MACEWEN

Sand dunes, interminable deserts, burning winds
the night temperature bitter, a land of grit;
and floating above me stars as violent
as fire balloons, tactile and brilliant.
The all-enveloping sky, a cloak of soot.
This is my story, my brief biography.
The sum total of my experience. I travel—
a compass useless in my useless hand—
through a sandscape, a singular topography.
I am a continent, a violated geography.

Restless in all this emptiness, I seek
a fellow traveler, search for a sign—
a secret handshake, a phrase, some unusual color
like periwinkle, for instance, or bright citrine,
but the monotony of sand persists
and nothing improbable finds entry
into the appalling platitudes of speech—
the *lingua franca* of everyone I meet—
in this land devoid of flags and pageantry.
Yet still I journey to this naked country,

for something in its nakedness has a beauty
so pure it's as if I thrust a knife
into my immaculate flesh and drew it forth
without a drop of blood being spilled. It is
abstract and invisible as air
this empty geometry, this ampersand
upon ampersand that leads me on
as if I were zero or the minus sign,
through "and," and "and," and "and,"
to seek a form which dances in the sand.

But nothing formal dances. Only the wind
blows—unchoreographed—a floating ghost
across the dunes. The sand, molecular,
airborne and free, is faint with the scent
of absolute dryness, a small mineral smell.
And this almost scentlessness, this shape without shape
is a violated country, one in which
I am both exile and inhabitant
and though I would escape
this is my chosen landscape.

May 2007

THEODORE ROETHKE

Florist's Root Cellar

Nothing would sleep in that cellar, dank as a ditch,
Bulbs broke out of boxes hunting for chinks in the dark,
Shoots dangled and drooped,
Lolling obscenely from mildewed crates,
Hung down long yellow evil necks, like tropical snakes.
And what a congress of stinks!—
Roots ripe as old bait,
Pulpy stems, rank, silo-rich,
Leaf-mould, manure, lime, piled against slippery planks.
Nothing would give up life:
Even the dirt kept breathing a small breath.

November 1943

Good descriptive poems are like perfumes made tactile.

W. S. DI PIERO, January 2006

In poems as elsewhere, a description is, like it or not, made use of, to speak of worlds and to live in them.

ROBERT CREELEY, June 1961

WALLACE STEVENS

Tea at the Palaz of Hoon

Not less because in purple I descended
The western day through what you called
The loneliest air, not less was I myself.

What was the ointment sprinkled on my beard?
What were the hymns that buzzed beside my ears?
What was the sea whose tide swept through me there?

Out of my mind the golden ointment rained,
And my ears made the blowing hymns they heard.
I was myself the compass of that sea:

I was the world in which I walked, and what I saw
Or heard or felt came not from myself;
And there I found myself more truly and more strange.

October 1921

BASIL BUNTING

From Briggflatts

Brag, sweet tenor bull,
descant on Rawthey's madrigal,
each pebble its part
for the fells' late spring.
Dance tiptoe, bull,
black against may.
Ridiculous and lovely
chase hurdling shadows
morning into noon.
May on the bull's hide
and through the dale
furrows fill with may,
paving the slowworm's way.

A mason times his mallet
to a lark's twitter,
listening while the marble rests,
lays his rule
at a letter's edge,
fingertips checking,
till the stone spells a name
naming none,
a man abolished.
Painful lark, labouring to rise!
The solemn mallet says:
In the grave's slot
he lies. We rot.

Decay thrusts the blade,
wheat stands in excrement
trembling. Rawthey trembles.
Tongue stumbles, ears err
for fear of spring.
Rub the stone with sand,
wet sandstone rending
roughness away. Fingers
ache on the rubbing stone.
The mason says: Rocks
happen by chance.
No one here bolts the door,
love is so sore.

Stone smooth as skin,
cold as the dead they load
on a low lorry by night.
The moon sits on the fell
but it will rain.
Under sacks on the stone
two children lie,
hear the horse stale,
the mason whistle,
harness mutter to shaft,
felloe to axle squeak,
rut thud the rim,
crushed grit.

Stocking to stocking, jersey to jersey,
head to a hard arm,
they kiss under the rain,
bruised by their marble bed.
In Garsdale, dawn;
at Hawes, tea from the can.
Rain stops, sacks
steam in the sun, they sit up.
Copper-wire moustache,
sea-reflecting eyes
and Baltic plainsong speech
declare: By such rocks
men killed Bloodaxe.

Fierce blood throbs in his tongue,
lean words.
Skulls cropped for steel caps
huddle round Stainmore.
Their becks ring on limestone,
whisper to peat.
The clogged cart pushes the horse downhill.
In such soft air
they trudge and sing,
laying the tune frankly on the air.
All sounds fall still,
fellside bleat,
hide-and-seek peewit.

Her pulse their pace,
palm countering palm,
till a trench is filled,
stone white as cheese
jeers at the dale.
Knotty wood, hard to rive,
smoulders to ash;
smell of October apples.
The road again,
at a trot.
Wetter, warmed, they watch
the mason meditate
on name and date.

Rain rinses the road,
the bull streams and laments.
Sour rye porridge from the hob
with cream and black tea,
meat, crust and crumb.
Her parents in bed
the children dry their clothes.
He has untied the tape
of her striped flannel drawers
before the range. Naked
on the pricked rag mat
his fingers comb
thatch of his manhood's home.

Gentle generous voices weave
over bare night
words to confirm and delight
till bird dawn.
Rainwater from the butt
she fetches and flannel
to wash him inch by inch,
kissing the pebbles.
Shining slowworm part of the marvel.
The mason stirs:
Words!
Pens are too light.
Take a chisel to write.

Every birth a crime,
every sentence life.
Wiped of mould and mites
would the ball run true?
No hope of going back.
Hounds falter and stray,
shame deflects the pen.
Love murdered neither bleeds nor stifles
but jogs the draftsman's elbow.
What can he, changed, tell
her, changed, perhaps dead?
Delight dwindles. Blame
stays the same.

Brief words are hard to find,
shapes to carve and discard:
Bloodaxe, king of York,
king of Dublin, king of Orkney.
Take no notice of tears;
letter the stone to stand
over love laid aside lest
insufferable happiness impede
flight to Stainmore,
to trace
lark, mallet,
becks, flocks
and axe knocks.

Dung will not soil the slowworm's
mosaic. Breathless lark
drops to nest in sodden trash;
Rawthey truculent, dingy.
Drudge at the mallet, the may is down,
fog on fells. Guilty of spring
and spring's ending
amputated years ache after
the bull is beef, love a convenience.
It is easier to die than to remember.
Name and date
split in soft slate
a few months obliterate.

January 1966

Night

The cold remote islands
And the blue estuaries
Where what breathes, breathes
The restless wind of the inlets,
And what drinks, drinks
The incoming tide;

Where shell and weed
Wait upon the salt wash of the sea,
And the clear nights of stars
Swing their lights westward
To set behind the land;

Where the pulse clinging to the rocks
Renews itself forever;
Where, again on unclouded nights,
The water reflects
The firmament's partial setting;

—O remember
In your narrowing dark hours
That more things move
Than blood in the heart.

October 1962

RODNEY JACK

After the Diagnosis

They erected a chainlink fence around
Peachtree Mortgage & Loan,
the building I once climbed
by way of a drainpipe and a tree-of-heaven
to the hot tar top, closer to a box maple's
topmost bejeweled branches—laden with samaras.

Stomping through a plush rug
of creeper and fallen sourwood flowers, I know
that I'm alive—as Darwin described it:
greedily hungry, fit to survive—
not the least bit concerned with fences.

I scale the chainlink, then the building,
sit on the roof dreaming
of my future house: vaulted ceilings,
walls mostly windows looking out to a yard

lush with royal paulownia, black locust,
angelhair also known as mimosa—
those trees like weeds that grow where they can,
beside a dumpster, gutter, punched through
a sidewalk crack, whose numbers
are legion and whose flowers are proud,
like the sourwood lilies I tread on my way home.

May 1999

MARGARET ATWOOD

Pig Song

This is what you changed me to:
a greypink vegetable with slug
eyes, buttock
incarnate, spreading like a slow turnip,

a skin you stuff so you may feed
in your turn, a stinking wart
of flesh, a large tuber
of blood which munches
and bloats. Very well then. Meanwhile

I have the sky, which is only half
caged, I have my weed corners,
I keep myself busy, singing
my song of roots and noses,

my song of dung. Madame,
this song offends you, these grunts
which you find oppressively sexual,
mistaking simple greed for lust.

I am yours. If you feed me garbage,
I will sing a song of garbage.
This is a hymn.

February 1974

What the old have come to disregard, the young inherit and make use of.

WALLACE STEVENS to HARRIET MONROE, June 23, 1915

Blues Alabama

She's blacker
than the night which holds
us in our communion
against the white picket fences.
There's clash in her eyes,
and she smiles whitely
to the tambourines.
There's a folk song audience
of rebels who lover
her mother into children,
and they're all in the roads
searching for the art
which makes singing
a blessing of hatred.

February 1968

ISAAC ROSENBERG

Break of Day in the Trenches

The darkness crumbles away—
It is the same old Druid Time as ever.
Only a live thing leaps my hand—
A queer sardonic rat—
As I pull the parapet's poppy
To stick behind my ear.
Droll rat, they would shoot you if they knew
Your cosmopolitan sympathies
(And God knows what antipathies).
Now you have touched this English hand
You will do the same to a German—
Soon, no doubt, if it be your pleasure
To cross the sleeping green between.
It seems you inwardly grin as you pass:
Strong eyes, fine limbs, haughty athletes,
Less chanced than you for life;
Bonds to the whims of murder,
Sprawled in the bowels of the earth,
The torn fields of France.
What do you see in our eyes
At the boom, the hiss, the swiftness,
The irrevocable earth buffet—
A shell's haphazard fury.
What rootless poppies dropping? . . . . .
But mine in my ear is safe,
Just a little white with the dust.

December 1916

Of Late

"Stephen Smith, University of Iowa sophomore, burned what he
    said was his draft card."
And Norman Morrison, Quaker, of Baltimore Maryland, burned
    what he said was himself.
You, Robert McNamara, burned what you said was a concentration
of the enemy aggressor.
No news medium troubled to put it in quotes.

And Norman Morrison, Quaker, of Baltimore Maryland, burned
    what he said was himself.
He said it with simple materials such as would be found in your
    kitchen.
In your office you were informed.
Reporters got cracking frantically on the mental disturbance angle.
So far nothing turns up.

Norman Morrison, Quaker, of Baltimore Maryland, burned, and
    while burning, screamed.
No tip-off. No release.
Nothing to quote, to manage to put in quotes.
Pity the unaccustomed hesitance of the newspaper editorialists.
Pity the press photographers, not called.

Norman Morrison, Quaker, of Baltimore Maryland, burned and
    was burned and said
all that there is to say in that language.
Twice what is said in yours.
It is a strange sect, Mr. McNamara, under advice to try
the whole of a thought in silence, and to oneself.

October 1966

RANDALL JARRELL

Protocols

(Birkenau, Odessa)

We went there on the train. *They had big barges that they towed,*
We stood up, there were so many I was squashed.
There was a smoke-stack, then they made me wash,
It was a factory, I think. *My mother held me up*
And I could see the ship that made the smoke.

When I was tired my mother carried me.
She said, "Don't be afraid." But I was only tired.
Where we went there is no more Odessa.
They had water in a pipe—like rain, but hot;
The water there is deeper than the world

And I was tired and fell in in my sleep
And the water drank me. That is what I think.
And I said to my mother, "Now I'm washed and dried,"
My mother hugged me, and it smelled like hay
And that is how you die. And that is how you die.

June 1945

TOM DISCH

The Prisoners of War

Their language disappeared a year or so
after the landscape: so what can they do now
but point? At parts of bodies, at what
they want to eat, at instrument panels, at
new highways and other areas of intense
reconstruction, at our own children smiling
into cameras, at the lettering on cannisters,
at streaks of green and purple, at the moon,
at moments that may still suggest such concepts
as "Civilization" or "Justice" or "Terror,"
and at ourselves, those still alive, who stand
before what might have been, a year ago, a door.

September 1972

Shelter the refugee Muses for a time.

RUPERT BROOKE to HARRIET MONROE, October 28, 1914

There's not a soul who cares twopence what I or any other poet thinks about the war. . . . We are experts on nothing but arrangements and patterns of vowels and consonants, and every time we shout about something else we increase the contempt the public has for us. We are entitled to the same voice as anybody else with a vote, no more. To claim more is arrogant.

BASIL BUNTING, September 1972

A Dog Was Crying To-Night in Wicklow Also

In memory of Donatus Nwoga

When human beings found out about death
They sent the dog to Chukwu with a message:
They wanted to be let back to the house of life.
They didn't want to end up lost forever
Like burnt wood disappearing into smoke
Or ashes that get blown away to nothing.
Instead, they saw their souls in a flock at twilight
Cawing and headed back for the same old roosts
And the same bright airs and wing-stretchings each morning.
Death would be like a night spent in the wood:
At first light they'd be back in the house of life.
(The dog was meant to tell all this to Chukwu.)

But death and human beings took second place
When he trotted off the path and started barking
At another dog in broad daylight just barking
Back at him from the far bank of a river.

And that is how the toad reached Chukwu first,
The toad who'd overheard in the beginning
What the dog was meant to tell. "Human beings," he said
(And here the toad was trusted absolutely),
"Human beings want death to last forever."

Then Chukwu saw the people's souls in birds
Coming towards him like black spots off the sunset
To a place where there would be neither roosts nor trees
Nor any way back to the house of life.
And his mind reddened and darkened all at once
And nothing that the dog would tell him later
Could change that vision. Great chiefs and great loves
In obliterated light, the toad in mud,
The dog crying out all night behind the corpse house.

October/November 1995

HART CRANE

At Melville's Tomb

Often beneath the wave, wide from this ledge,
The dice of drowned men's bones he saw bequeath
An embassy. Their numbers, as he watched,
Beat on the dusty shore and were obscured.

And wrecks passed without sound of bells,
The calyx of death's bounty giving back
A scattered chapter, livid hieroglyph,
The portent wound in corridors of shells.

Then in the circuit calm of one vast coil,
Its lashings charmed and malice reconciled,
Frosted eyes there were that lifted altars:
And silent answers crept across the stars.

Compass, quadrant and sextant contrive
No farther tides . . . . High in the azure steeps
Monody shall not wake the mariner.
This fabulous shadow only the sea keeps.

October 1926

O Daedalus, Fly Away Home

*"Lots uh slaves wut wuz brung ovuh from Africa could fly . . . Dey
dohn like it heah . . . an go back to Africa . . ."*
LEGEND OF THE FLYING AFRICAN

Drifting scent of the Georgia pines,
coonskin drum and jubilee banjo.
   Pretty Malinda, dance with me.

Night is juba, night is conjo,
   Pretty Malinda, dance with me. . . .

Night is an African juju man
weaving a wish and a weariness together
to make two wings.

   O fly away home, fly away.

Do you remember Africa?

   O cleave the air, fly away home.

I knew all the stars of Africa.

   Spread my wings and cleave the air.

My gran, he flew back to Africa,
just spread his arms and flew away home. . . .

Drifting night in the windy pines,
Night is a laughing, night is a longing.
   Dusk-rose Malinda, come to me. . . .

Night is a mourning juju man
weaving a wish and a weariness together
to make two wings.

   O fly away home, fly away.

                    July 1943

CHARLES BUKOWSKI

A Not So Good Night in the San Pedro of the World

it's unlikely that a decent poem is in me
tonight
and I understand that this is strictly my
problem
and of no interest to you
that I sit here listening to a man playing
a piano on the radio
and it's bad piano, both the playing and
the composition
and again, this is of no interest to you
as one of my cats,
a beautiful white with strange markings,
sleeps in the bathroom.

I have no idea of what would be of
interest to you
but I doubt that you would be of
interest to me, so don't get
superior.
in fact, come to think of it, you can
kiss my ass.

I continue to listen to the piano.
this will not be a memorable night in my
life
or yours.

let us celebrate the stupidity of our
endurance.

September 1993

ADRIENNE RICH

Final Notations

it will not be simple, it will not be long
it will take little time, it will take all your thought
it will take all your heart, it will take all your breath
it will be short, it will not be simple

it will touch through your ribs, it will take all your heart
it will not be long, it will occupy your thought
as a city is occupied, as a bed is occupied
it will take all your flesh, it will not be simple

You are coming into us who cannot withstand you
you are coming into us who never wanted to withstand you
you are taking parts of us into places never planned
you are going far away with pieces of our lives

it will be short, it will take all your breath
it will not be simple, it will become your will

September 1991

People that read without an abundance of love leave the book they have read as famished as they were before they came to it. . . . How easy it is to go to a great poet with a small listless heart, and with morose surd ears; for though the arbute shakes in the wind, the eye is lookless, and though the kelp has the acutest longing for the sea in it, the nose is stupid, and the dells and hard frith that are signs of the opaque substance of mortal will are dead dirt. There is a secret, porcine disgrace in loveless reading, just as there is in any instant of our lives when we are not remembering actively, and our thoughts are of starvelled material, and our passions are not the gems that were on Aaron's breastplate, but just rubble and slain stones.

EDWARD DAHLBERG, April 1951

The Shield of Achilles

> She looked over his shoulder
>   For vines and olive trees,
> Marble, well-governed cities
>   And ships upon wine-dark seas;
> But there on the shining metal
>   His hands had put instead
> An artificial wilderness
>   And a sky like lead.

A plain without a feature, bare and brown,
  No blade of grass, no sign of neighborhood,
Nothing to eat and nowhere to sit down;
  Yet, congregated on that blankness, stood
  An unintelligible multitude,
A million eyes, a million boots, in line,
Without expression, waiting for a sign.

Out of the air a voice without a face
  Proved by statistics that some cause was just
In tones as dry and level as the place;
  No one was cheered and nothing was discussed,
  Column by column, in a cloud of dust,
They marched away, enduring a belief
Whose logic brought them, somewhere else, to grief.

> She looked over his shoulder
>   For ritual pieties,
> White flower-garlanded heifers,
>   Libation and sacrifice:
> But there on the shining metal
>   Where the altar should have been
> She saw by his flickering forge-light
>   Quite another scene.

Barbed wire enclosed an arbitrary spot
    Where bored officials lounged (one cracked a joke)
And sentries sweated for the day was hot;
    A crowd of ordinary decent folk
    Watched from outside and neither moved nor spoke
As three pale figures were led forth and bound
To three posts driven upright in the ground.

The mass and majesty of this world, all
    That carries weight and always weighs the same,
Lay in the hands of others; they were small
    And could not hope for help, and no help came;
    What their foes liked to do was done; their shame
Was all the worst could wish: they lost their pride
And died as men before their bodies died.

        She looked over his shoulder
           For athletes at their games,
        Men and women in a dance
           Moving their sweet limbs,
        Quick, quick, to music;
           But there on the shining shield
        His hands set no dancing-floor
           But a weed-choked field.

A ragged urchin, aimless and alone,
    Loitered about that vacancy; a bird
Flew up to safety from his well-aimed stone:
    That girls are raped, that two boys knife a third,
    Were axioms to him, who'd never heard
Of any world where promises were kept
Or one could weep because another wept.

The thin-lipped armorer
   Hephaestos hobbled away;
Thetis of the shining breasts
   Cried out in dismay
At what the God had wrought
   To please her son, the strong
Iron-hearted man-slaying Achilles
   Who would not live long.

October 1952

ALBERT GOLDBARTH

He Has

the high-boned taut-toned moody ink-eyes beauty
some men lead a girl to hell with whistling all the while.
Or say her every step displays the little jumpstart jazz
in her ass that a boy's gaze superglues to, even over
broken glass, humiliation, fiscal ruin. The eye
betrays us daily. The eye, and the frame we bring
to our seeing. On the beach: that beautiful cartouche
of raw-sienna feathering and pucker is—*step back*—
the fatal sear of a jellyfish whip across the chest
of one more luckless tourist. Try to tell her husband
how museum-worthy you find the design of her death.
Is the beauty the glutinous spiral of fish guts;
or the voluminous screw-thread spiraling-down of the gulls
to gorge? Proximity determines so much.
When you're twelve you dream of "going to war,"
and not of it coming to you.

November 2006

ALICE FULTON

What I Like

Friend—the face I wallow toward
through a scrimmage of shut faces.
Arms like towropes to haul me home, aide-
memoire, my lost childhood docks, a bottled ark
in harbor. *Friend*—I can't forget
how even the word contains an *end*.
We circle each other in scared bolero,
imagining strategems: postures and imposters.
Cold convictions keep us solo. I ahem
and hedge my affections. Who'll blow the first kiss,
land it like the lifeforces we feel,
tickling at each wrist? It should be easy
easy to take your hand, whisper down this distance
labeled hers or his: what I like about you is

January 1983

Rendezvous

Not for these lovely blooms that prank your chambers did I come. Indeed,
I could have loved you better in the dark;
That is to say, in rooms less bright with roses, rooms more casual, less aware
Of History in the wings about to enter with benevolent air
On ponderous tiptoe, at the cue "Proceed."
Not that I like the ash-trays over-crowded and the place in a mess,
Or the monastic cubicle too unctuously austere and stark,
But partly that these formal garlands for our Eighth Street Aphrodite are a bit too Greek,
And partly that to make the poor walls rich with our unaided loveliness
Would have been more *chic*.

Yet here I am, having told you of my quarrel with the taxi-driver over a line of Milton, and you laugh; and you are you, none other.
Your laughter pelts my skin with small delicious blows.
But I am perverse: I wish you had not scrubbed—with pumice, I suppose—
The tobacco stains from your beautiful fingers. And I wish I did not feel like your mother.

May 1939

Fever 103°

Pure? What does it mean?
The tongues of hell
Are dull, dull as the triple

Tongues of dull, fat Cerberus
Who wheezes at the gate. Incapable
Of licking clean

The aguey tendon, the sin, the sin.
The tinder cries.
The indelible smell

Of a snuffed candle!
Love, love, the low smokes roll
From me like Isadora's scarves, I'm in a fright

One scarf will catch and anchor in the wheel,
Such yellow sullen smokes
Make their own element. They will not rise,

But trundle round the globe
Choking the aged and the meek,
The weak

Hothouse baby in its crib,
The ghastly orchid
Hanging its hanging garden in the air,

Devilish leopard!
Radiation turned it white
And killed it in an hour.

Greasing the bodies of adulterers
Like Hiroshima ash and eating in.
The sin. The sin.

Darling, all night
I have been flickering, off, on, off, on.
The sheets grow heavy as a lecher's kiss.

Three days. Three nights.
Lemon water, chicken
Water, water make me retch.

I am too pure for you or anyone.
Your body
Hurts me as the world hurts God. I am a lantern—

My head a moon
Of Japanese paper, my gold beaten skin
Infinitely delicate and infinitely expensive.

Does not my heat astound you! And my light!
All by myself I am a huge camellia
Glowing and coming and going, flush on flush.

I think I am going up,
I think I may rise—
The beads of hot metal fly, and I love, I

Am a pure acetylene
Virgin
Attended by roses,

By kisses, by cherubim,
By whatever these pink things mean!
Not you, nor him

Nor him, nor him
(My selves dissolving, old whore petticoats)—
To Paradise.

August 1963

It is obviously important to discover who "we" are supposed to be, who know these bitter things, that art is a fake but when vital has death somewhere at its roots.

HUGH KENNER, December 1955

Poems—letters to friends and enemies, to the dead, maybe to one living person.

ANNA KAMIENSKA, June 2010

LISEL MUELLER

In the Thriving Season

Now as she catches fistfuls of sun
riding down dust and air to her crib,
my first child in her first spring
stretches bare hands back to your darkness
and heals your silence, the vast hurt
of your deaf ear and mute tongue
with doves hatched in her young throat.

Now ghost-begotten infancies
are the marrow of trees and pools
and blue uprisings in the woods
spread revolution to the mind,
I can believe birth is fathered
by death, believe that she was quick
when you forgave pain and terror
and shook the fever from your blood.

Now in the thriving season of love
when the bud relents into flower,
your love turned absence has turned once more,
and if my comforts fall soft as rain
on her flutters, it is because
love grows by what it remembers of love.

August 1959

Magnificat

When he had suckled there, he began
to grow: first, he was an infant in her arms,
but soon, drinking and drinking at the sweet
milk she could not keep from filling her,
from pouring into his ravenous mouth,
and filling again, miraculous pitcher, mercy
feeding its own extinction . . . soon he was
huge, towering above her, the landscape,
his shadow stealing the color from the fields,
even the flowers going gray. And they came
like ants, one behind the next, to worship
him—huge as he was, and hungry; it was
his hunger they admired most of all.
So they brought him slaughtered beasts:
goats, oxen, bulls, and finally, their own
kin whose hunger was a kind of shame
to them, a shrinkage; even as his was
beautiful to them, magnified, magnificent.

The day came when they had nothing left
to offer him, having denuded themselves
of all in order to enlarge him, in whose
shadow they dreamed of light: and that
is when the thought began to move, small
at first, a whisper, then a buzz, and finally,
it broke out into words, so loud they thought
it must be prophecy: they would kill him,
and all they had lost in his name would return,
renewed and fresh with the dew of morning.
Hope fed their rage, sharpened their weapons.

And who is she, hooded figure, mourner now
at the fate of what she fed? And the slow rain,
which never ends, who is the father of that?
And who are we who speak, as if the world
were our diorama—its little figures moved
by hidden gears, precious in miniature, tin soldiers,
spears the size of pins, perfect replicas, history
under glass, dusty, old fashioned, a curiosity
that no one any longer wants to see,
excited as they are by the new giant, who feeds
on air, grows daily on radio waves, in cyberspace,
who sows darkness like a desert storm,
who blows like a wind through the Boardrooms,
who touches the hills, and they smoke.

August 2004

ATSURO RILEY

Hutch

—by way of what they say

From back when it was Nam time I tell you what.

Them days men boys gone dark groves rose like Vietnam bamboo.

Aftergrowth something awful.

Green have mercy souls here seen camouflage everlasting.

Nary a one of the brung-homes brung home whole.

Mongst tar-pines come upon this box-thing worked from scrapwood.

Puts me much myself in mind of a rabbit-crouch.

Is it more a meat-safe.

Set there hid bedded there looking all the world like a coffin.

Somebody cares to tend to it like a spring gets tendered clears the leaves!

Whosoever built it set wire window-screen down the sides.

Long about five foot or thereabouts close kin to a dog-crate.

A human would have to hunch.

Closes over heavy this hingey-type lid on it like a casket.

Swearing to Jesus wadn't it eye-of-pine laid down for the floor.

Remembering the Garner twins Carl and Charlie come home mute.

Cherry-bombs 4th of July them both belly-scuttling under the house.

Their crave of pent-places ditchpipes.

Mongst tar-pines come upon this box-thing worked from scrapwood.

From back when it was Nam time I tell you what.

December 2007

Or,

Or Oreo, or
worse. Or ordinary.
Or your choice
of category

or
Color

or any color
other than Colored
or Colored Only.
Or "Of Color"

or
Other

or theory or discourse
or oral territory.
Oregon or Georgia
or Florida Zora

or
Opportunity

or born poor
or Corporate. Or Moor.
Or a Noir Orpheus
or Senghor

or
Diaspora

or a horrendous
and tore-up journey.
Or performance. Or allegory's armor
of ignorant comfort

     or
     Worship

or reform or a sore chorus.
Or Electoral Corruption
or important ports
of Yoruba or worry

     or
     Neighbor

or fear of . . .
of terror or border.
Or all organized
minorities.

October 2006

No Swan So Fine

"No water so still as the
    dead fountains of Versailles." No swan,
with swart blind look askance
and ambidextrous legs, so fine
    as the chintz china one with fawn-
brown eyes and toothed gold
    collar on to show whose bird it was.

Lodged in the Louis Fifteenth
    candelabrum-tree of cockscomb-
tinted buttons, dahlias,
sea-urchins and everlastings,
    it perches on the branching foam
of polished sculptured
flowers—at ease and tall. The king is dead.

October 1932

The Traveler

They pointed me out on the highway, and they said
'That man has a curious way of holding his head.'

They pointed me out on the beach; they said 'That man
Will never become as we are, try as he can.'

They pointed me out at the station, and the guard
Looked at me twice, thrice, thoughtfully & hard.

I took the same train that the others took,
To the same place. Were it not for that look
And those words, we were all of us the same.
I studied merely maps. I tried to name
The effects of motion on the travelers,
I watched the couple I could see, the curse
And blessings of that couple, their destination,
The deception practised on them at the station,
Their courage. When the train stopped and they knew
The end of their journey, I descended too.

April 1948

AVERILL CURDY

Sparrow Trapped in the Airport

Never the bark and abalone mask
cracked by storms of a mastering god,
never the gods' favored glamour, never
the pelagic messenger bearing orchards
in its beak, never allegory, not wisdom
or valor or cunning, much less hunger
demanding vigilance, industry, invention,
or the instinct to claim some small rise
above the plain and from there to assert
the song of another day ending;
lentil brown, uncounted, overlooked
in the clamorous public of the flock
so unlikely to be noticed here by arrivals,
faces shining with oils of their many miles,
where it hops and scratches below
the baggage carousel and lights too high,
too bright for any real illumination,
looking more like a fumbled punch line
than a stowaway whose revelation
recalls how lightly we once traveled.

November 2005

We are most original when we are most like life. Life is the natural thing. Interpretation is the factitious. Nature is always variable. To have an eye with brain in it—that is, or rather would be, the poetic millenium. We are not moonlit strummers now: we are gun-pointers and sky-climbers.

MARSDEN HARTLEY, December 1919

His Presence

I foreswore red wine
and the white;
I was whole,
I foreswore lover and love;
all delight
must come,
I had said,
of the soul;
I waited impassioned,
alone and alert
in the night:
did he come?

I foreswore child and my home;
I said,
I will walk
to his most distant wood
for his laurel;
I wandered alone;
I said,
on the height I will find him;
I said,
he will come with the red
first pure light of the sun.

I read volume and tome
of old magic,
I made sign and cross-sign;
he must answer old magic;
he must know the old symbol:
I swear I will find him,
I will bind
his power in a faggot,
a tree,
a stone,
or a bush or a jar
of well-water,
I went far
to old pilgrim sites
for that water;

I entreated the grove and the spring,
the bay-tree in flower;
I was wise on my way,
they said I was wise,
I was steeped in their lore,
I entreated his love,
I prayed him each hour;
I was sterile
and barren
and songless.

I came back:
he opened my door.

March 1933

RAE ARMANTROUT

Transactions

1

What do we like best
about ourselves?

Our inability
to be content.

We might see this
restlessness

as a chip
not yet cashed in.

2

You appear
because you're lonely

maybe.
You would not say that.

You come to tell me
you're saving money
by cooking for yourself.

You've figured out
what units you'll need

to exchange for units
if you intend

I know I mustn't
interrupt

3

Hectic and flexible,

flames

are ideal

new bodies for us!

October 2011

The Children of the Poor

1

People who have no children can be hard:
Attain a mail of ice and insolence:
Need not pause in the fire, and in no sense
Hesitate in the hurricane to guard.
And when wide world is bitten and bewarred
They perish purely, waving their spirits hence
Without a trace of grace or of offense
To laugh or fail, diffident, wonder-starred.
While through a throttling dark we others hear
The little lifting helplessness, the queer
Whimper-whine; whose unridiculous
Lost softness softly makes a trap for us.
And makes a curse. And makes a sugar of
The malocclusions, the inconditions of love.

2

What shall I give my children? who are poor,
Who are adjudged the leastwise of the land,
Who are my sweetest lepers, who demand
No velvet and no velvety velour;
But who have begged me for a brisk contour,
Crying that they are quasi, contraband
Because unfinished, graven by a hand
Less than angelic, admirable or sure.
My hand is stuffed with mode, design, device.
But I lack access to my proper stone.
And plenitude of plan shall not suffice
Nor grief nor love shall be enough alone
To ratify my little halves who bear
Across an autumn freezing everywhere.

And shall I prime my children, pray, to pray?
Mites, come invade most frugal vestibules
Spectered with crusts of penitents' renewals
And all hysterics arrogant for a day.
Instruct yourselves here is no devil to pay.
Children, confine your lights in jellied rules;
Resemble graves; be metaphysical mules;
Learn Lord will not distort nor leave the fray.
Behind the scurryings of your neat motif
I shall wait, if you wish: revise the psalm
If that should frighten you: sew up belief
If that should tear: turn, singularly calm
At forehead and at fingers rather wise,
Holding the bandage ready for your eyes.

March 1949

E. E. CUMMINGS
What If a Much of a Which of a Wind

what if a much of a which of a wind
gives the truth to summer's lie;
bloodies with dizzying leaves the sun
and yanks immortal stars awry?
Blow king to beggar and queen to seem
(blow friend to fiend: blow space to time)
—when skies are hanged and oceans drowned,
the single secret will still be man

what if a keen of a lean wind flays
screaming hills with sleet and snow:
strangles valleys by ropes of thing
and stifles forests in white ago?
Blow hope to terror; blow seeing to blind
(blow pity to envy and soul to mind)
—whose hearts are mountains, roots are trees,
it's they shall cry hello to the spring

what if a dawn of a doom of a dream
bites this universe in two,
peels forever out of his grave
and sprinkles nowhere with me and you?
Blow soon to never and never to twice
(blow life to isn't: blow death to was)
—all nothing's only our hugest home;
the most who die, the more we live

July 1943

Mu'allaqa

The elephant's trunk uncurling
From the lightning flashes
In the clouds was Marie Antoinette,
As usual trumpeting.
The greedy suction
Was her tornado vacuuming across the golden Kansas flatness.

Meanwhile, the count was talking to the swan.
The swan liked what he was saying and got
Right out of the pond.
Meanwhile, grown men in Afghanistan.
The count had fought in Algeria.
Meanwhile, neon in Tokyo.

Madame la Comtesse waved to us from the top step,
Waved to her count, their swan, their ornamental pond, *et moi.*
We were a towering cornucopia
Of autumn happiness
And *gourmandise* rotating counterclockwise,
Backwards toward the guillotine.

I kept a rainbow as a pet and grandly
Walked the rainbow on a leash.
I exercised it evenings together with the cheetah,
A Thorstein Veblen moment of conspicuous consumption:
A dapper dauphin in a T-shirt that said FRED
Parading with his pets decked out in T-shirts that said FRED's.

Note: "Mu'allaqa" is a tribute to the Arab poet Imru' al-Qays and his collection of poems known as the Mu'allaqat.

I left my liver in the Cher.
I ate my heart out *en Berry*.
We drank and ate
France between the wars,
And every morning couldn't wait.
It felt sunshiny in the shadow of the château.

And when the rainbow leapt from there to here,
It landed twenty years away from the Cher.
The place it landed was the Persian Gulf.
It landed twinkling stardust where I'm standing in my life
With one-hump Marie Antoinette, my wife,
Who resembles that disarming camel yesterday.

In fact, the camel yesterday was smitten.
She left the other camels to come over.
You have a lovely liquid wraparound eye.
She stood there looking at me sideways.
They feed their racing camels caviar in Qatar.
The ruler of Dubai has said that he will try to buy Versailles.

A refrigerated ski slope, five stories high,
Lives improbably inside a downtown shopping mall in Dubai.
Arab men, wearing sneakers under their robes, hold hands.
Faceless black veils stop shopping to watch through the glass.
Seeing the skiers emphasizes the desert,
Like hearing far-off thunder at a picnic.

Both the word *thunder* and the word *picnic* are of course Arabic.
Indeed, Arabic was the language of French aristocrats
Before the Terror, bad body odor perfumed.
It is the language of the great Robert Frost poems,
Which have the suicide bomber's innocence
Walking safely past the checkpoint into the crowd.

They pay payola to Al Qaeda to stay away from Doha.
The emir was in his counting-house, counting out his oil and gas.
Another sunny Sunni day in the UAE!
A candidate for president
Who wants to manumit our oil-dependent nation
First has to get the message to every oily girl and boy

To just say no to up and down and in and out, Labanotation
Of moaning oil rigs extracting oil joy.
My fellow Americans, I see a desert filled with derricks
Pumping up and down but never satisfied:
Obsessional hydraulics and Jimi Hendrix has hysterics.
I smash my guitar to bits on stage and that's all, folks!

It isn't.
I contemplate the end of the world. It isn't.
I have my croissant and café and the *Trib* and walk the rainbow
Around the block.
The young North African hipsters in the bitter *banlieues*
Contemplate the end of the world.

I contemplate the end of the world but in my case
It's not.
There are still things to buy.
I walk the rainbow in the dark.
The world is the kiosk where I get my *Herald Tribune*.
The world is my local café where my *café au lait* is quadroon.

I go to the strange little statue of Pierre Mendès-France
In the Jardin du Luxembourg, in Paris, France.
I make a pilgrimage to it.
My quaint political saint and I visit.
The young North African hipsters in the bitter *banlieues*
Contemplate the end of the world, which isn't

The end of the world, though yes, quite true,
In Algeria and Afghanistan
Jihad is developing a dirty nuclear bomb
That smells like frangipani in flower
To keep Frangipani in power.
Ayatollah Frangipani has returned from his long exile in France

To annihilate vice.
I stomp the campfire out and saddle up my loyal *Mayflower*—
Who is swifter than a life is brief under the stars!
My prize four-wheel-drive with liquid wraparound eyes!
We ski the roller coaster ocean's up and down dunes.
We reach land at last and step on Plymouth Rock.

April 2008

GEOFFREY HILL

The Peacock at Alderton

Nothing to tell why I cannot write
in re Nobody; nobody to narrate this
latter acknowledgement: the self that counts
words to a line, accountable survivor
pain-wedged, pinioned in the cleft trunk,
less petty than a sprite, poisonous as Ariel
to Prospero's own knowledge. In my room
a vase of peacock feathers. I will attempt
to describe them, as if for evidence
on which a life depends. Except for the eyes
they are threadbare: the threads hanging
from some luminate tough weed in February.
But those eyes—like a Greek letter,
omega, fossiled in an Indian shawl;
like a shaved cross-section of living tissue,
the edge metallic blue, the core of jet,
the white of the eye in fact closer to beige,
the whole encircled with a black-fringed green.
The peacock roosts alone on a Scots pine
at the garden end, in blustery twilight
his fulgent cloak a gathering of the dark,
the maharajah-bird that scavenges
close by the stone-troughed, stone-terraced, stone-ensurfed
Suffolk shoreline; at times displays his scream.

March 2007

It is for moments like this that one perseveres in [a] difficult poem, moments which would be less beautiful and meaningful if the rest did not exist, for we have fought side by side with the author in her struggle to achieve them.

JOHN ASHBERY, July 1957

A bad poem is full of English literature.

WILLIAM CARLOS WILLIAMS, July 1919

The best poetry has often been difficult, has often been so obscure that readers have fought passionately over it. The King James Bible comes closer to poetry than faith usually dares.

WILLIAM LOGAN, February 2006

MAY SWENSON

Green Red Brown and White

Bit an apple on its red
side   Smelled like snow
Between white halves broken open
brown winks slept in sockets of green

Stroked a birch white as a thigh
scar-flecked smooth as the neck
of a horse   On mossy pallets green
the pines dropped down
their perfect carvings brown

Lost in the hairy wood
followed berries red
to the fork   Had to choose
between green and green   High

in a sunwhite dome a brown bird
sneezed   Took the path least likely
and it led me home   For

each path leads both out and in
I come while going   No to and from
There is only here   And here
is as well as there   Wherever
I am led I move within the care
of the season
hidden in the creases of her skirts
of green or brown or beaded red

And when they are white
I am not lost   I am not lost then
only covered for the night

January 1951

ANNE STEVENSON

Inheriting My Grandmother's Nightmare

Consider the adhesiveness of things
    to the ghosts that prized them,
the "olden days" of birthday spoons
    and silver napkin rings.
Too carelessly I opened
    that velvet drawer of heirlooms.
There lay my grandmother's soul
begging under veils of tarnish to be brought back whole.

She who was always a climate in herself,
    who refused to vanish
as the nineteen-hundreds grew older and louder,
    and the wars worse,
and her grandchildren, bigger and ruder
    in her daughter's house.
How completely turned around
her lavender world became, how upside down.

And how much, under her "flyaway" hair,
    she must have suffered,
sitting there ignored by the dinner guests
    hour after candlelit hour,
rubbed out, like her initials on the silverware,
    eating little, passing bread,
until the wine's flood, the smoke's blast,
the thunderous guffaws at last roared her to bed.

In her tiny garden of confidence,
    wasted she felt, and furious.
She fled to church, but Baby Jesus
    had grown out of his manger.
She read of Jews in the *New Haven Register*
    gassed or buried alive.
Every night, at the wheel of an ambulance,
she drove and drove, not knowing how to drive.

She died in '55, paralyzed, helpless.
   Her no man's land survived.
I light my own age with a spill
   from her distress. And there it is,
her dream, my heirloom, my drive downhill
   at the wheel of the last bus,
the siren's wail, the smoke, the sickly smell.
The drawer won't shut again. It never will.

May 2007

Little Blessing for My Floater

After George Herbert

This tiny ruin in my eye, small
flaw in the fabric, little speck
of blood in the egg, deep chip
in the windshield, north star,
polestar, floater that doesn't
float, spot where my hand is not,
even when I'm looking at my hand,
little piton that nails every rock
I see, no matter if the picture
turns to sand, or sand to sea,
I embrace you, piece of absence
that reminds me what I will be,
all dark some day unless God
rescues me, oh speck
that might teach me yet to see.

November 2003

Prayer's End

Nature remains
        faithful by
                natural light,
only. Immeasurable,
        invisible in the wind.
                Visible when
blades
        and branches bend.
                The wind
speaks fluent
        rain. Despite it
                the rain
falls straight. And beyond it
abandoned barns
                defend
        abandoned
men.

November 2010

Who is the God lodged in my imagination? What do I make of it? Why is the first question inseparable from the second? Why am I glued to rivers and mountains, pristine or not? I hope my answers are ephemeral forms, poems that paradoxically make spaces as filled with flux as the world, and as the mind in the world, continually coming into being through a set of relations and then disintegrating.

EMILY WARN, April 2010

A religious devotion to the truth, to the splendor of the authentic, involves the writer in a process rewarding in itself; but when that devotion brings us to undreamed abysses and we find ourselves sailing slowly over them and landing on the other side—that's ecstasy.

DENISE LEVERTOV, September 1965

JACK SPICER

"Any fool can get into an ocean . . ."

Any fool can get into an ocean
But it takes a Goddess
To get out of one.
What's true of oceans is true, of course,
Of labyrinths and poems. When you start swimming
Through riptide of rhythms and the metaphor's seaweed
You need to be a good swimmer or a born Goddess
To get back out of them
Look at the sea otters bobbing wildly
Out in the middle of the poem
They look so eager and peaceful playing out there where
    the water hardly moves
You might get out through all the waves and rocks
Into the middle of the poem to touch them
But when you've tried the blessed water long
Enough to want to start backward
That's when the fun starts
Unless you're a poet or an otter or something supernatural
You'll drown, dear. You'll drown
Any Greek can get you into a labyrinth
But it takes a hero to get out of one
What's true of labyrinths is true of course
Of love and memory. When you start remembering.

July/August 2008

Fabrication of Ancestors

For old Billy Dugan, shot in the ass in the Civil War,
my father said.

The old wound in my ass
has opened up again, but I
am past the prodigies
of youth's campaigns, and weep
where I used to laugh
in war's red humors, half
in love with silly-assed pains
and half not feeling them.
I have to sit up with
an indoor, unsittable itch
before I go down late
and weeping to the storm-
cellar on a dirty night
and go to bed with the worms.
So pull the dirt up over me
and make a family joke
for Old Billy Blue Balls,
the oldest private in the world
with two ass-holes and no
place more to go to for a laugh
except the last one. Say:
The North won the Civil War
without much help from me
although I wear a proof
of the war's obscenity.

October/November 1962

EDWARD DORN

Dark Ceiling

Broad black scar the valley is
and sunday is
where
      in the wide arc
   the small lights of homes come on
in that trough.

   Burnish my heart
   with this mark

Furnish my soul with the hope
Far away and by a river
In the darkness of a walnut stand.

There
     is
no home, no back.

All is this wrong key, the lark
sings
     but his voice trails off
in the snow. He has not
brought his meadow.
The starling's
   insolent whistle
is the truth here—dark smoke

drifts in from the morning fertilizer factory
and men there return lamely
to work, their disputes not settled.

February 1964

Search Party

By now I know most of the faces
that will appear beside me as
long as there are still images
I know at last what I would choose
the next time if there ever was
a time again I know the days
that open in the dark like this
I do not know where Maoli is

I know the summer surfaces
of bodies and the tips of voices
like stars out of their distances
and where the music turns to noise
I know the bargains in the news
rules whole languages formulas
wisdom that I will never use
I do not know where Maoli is

I know whatever one may lose
somebody will be there who says
what it will be all right to miss
and what is verging on excess
I know the shadows of the house
routes that lead out to no traces
many of his empty places
I do not know where Maoli is

You that see now with your own eyes
all that there is as you suppose
though I could stare through broken glass
and show you where the morning goes
though I could follow to their close
the sparks of an exploding species
and see where the world ends in ice
I would not know where Maoli is

February 1992

LORINE NIEDECKER

Three Poems

I

River-marsh-drowse
and in flood
    moonlight
       gives sight
of no land.

They fish, a man
takes his wife to town
with his rowboat's 10-horse
    ships his voice
to the herons.

Sure they drink
—full foamy folk—
    till asleep.
   The place is asleep
on one leg in the weeds.

II

Property is poverty—
I've foreclosed.
I own again

these walls thin
as the back
of my writing tablet.

And more:
all who live here—
card table to eat on,

broken bed—
sacrifice for less
than art.

III

Now in one year
   a book published
      and plumbing—
took a lifetime
    to weep
      a deep
        trickle

     August 1963

DENISE LEVERTOV

Our Bodies

Our bodies, still young under
the engraved anxiety of our
faces, and innocently

more expressive than faces:
nipples, navel, and pubic hair
make anyway a

sort of face: or taking
the rounded shadows at
breast, buttock, balls,

the plump of my belly, the
hollow of your
groin, as a constellation,

how it leans from earth to
dawn in a gesture of
play and

wise compassion—
nothing like this
comes to pass
in eyes or wistful
mouths.
   I have

a line or groove I love
runs down
my body from breastbone
to waist. It speaks of
eagerness, of
distance.

        Your long back,
the sand color and
how the bones show, say

what sky after sunset
almost white
over a deep woods to which

rooks are homing, says.

        October/November 1963

It's perfectly true that we don't, as a Public People, think anything of our history, let alone the past, the compulsion is always towards the future with all that hag-ridden idealism about a happier generation to come (to which, incidentally, we pass the buck too). And, ignoring the past, living for the future, what becomes of our present? The thing that it is, perhaps, ambiguously frenzied in the cities, monotonous and dull in the suburbs, chewed up in the maw of business which is, as Coolidge said, the business of everybody— America! But there is a league that has said otherwise. Go read them. Get down to the grain.

JEAN GARRIGUE, August 1957

JAMES WRIGHT

The Blessing

Just off the highway to Rochester, Minnesota,
Twilight bounds softly forth on the grass.
And the eyes of those two Indian ponies
Darken with kindness.
They have come gladly out of the willows
To welcome my friend and me.
We step over the barbed wire into the pasture
Where they have been grazing all day, alone.
They ripple tensely, they can hardly contain their happiness
That we have come.
They bow shyly as wet swans. They love each other.
There is no loneliness like theirs.
At home once more,
They begin munching the young tufts of spring in the darkness.
I would like to hold the slenderer one in my arms,
For she has walked over to me
And nuzzled my left hand.
She is black and white,
Her mane falls wild on her forehead,
And the light breeze moves me to caress her long ear
That is delicate as the skin over a girl's wrist.
Suddenly I realize
That if I stepped out of my body I would break
Into blossom.

March 1961

Grass on the Cliff

Under the house, between the road and the sea-cliff, bitter wild
   grass
Stands narrowed between the people and the storm.
The ocean winter after winter gnaws at its earth, the wheels and
   the feet
Summer after summer encroach and destroy.
Stubborn green life, for the cliff-eater I cannot comfort you,
   ignorant which color,
Gray-blue or pale-green, will please the late stars;
But laugh at the other, your seed shall enjoy wonderful vengeances
   and suck
The arteries and walk in triumph on the faces.

January 1928

W. S. DI PIERO

Big City Speech

Use me
Abuse me
    Turn wheels of fire
    on manhole hotheads

Sing me
Sour me
    Secrete dark matter's sheen
    on our smarting skin

Rise and shine
In puddle shallows
    under every Meryl Cheryl Caleb Syd
    somnambulists and sleepyheads

Wake us
Speak to us
    Bless what you've nurtured in your pits
    the rats voles roaches and all outlivers
    of your obscene ethic and politics

Crawl on us
Fall on us
    you elevations that break and vein
    down to sulfuric fiber-optic wrecks
    through drill-bit dirt to bedrock

Beat our brows
Flee our sorrows

Sleep tight with your ultraviolets
righteous mica and drainage seeps

your gorgeous color-chart container ships
and cab-top numbers squinting in the mist

June 2009

CID CORMAN

From "Cahoots"

There wasnt space
for two to pass
at one moment

and that moment
at Potniae.
Fate had spoken

And Fate followed
through at the cost
of the Other.

It takes a life
time's blindness to
see one's father.

    .   .   .

The way one
wood-dove—buzz
buzz—follows

another—
the slow low
repeat—the

twang of an
arrow—the
way she to

whom I smile
returns the
smile: the way.

    .   .   .

To come out
after a
long day's work

into snow—
the latest
version of

nothingness
and all so
light and crisp—

as if we're
the candles
on the cake.

February 1983

RICHARD WILBUR

Hamlen Brook

At the alder-darkened brink
Where the stream slows to a lucid jet
I lean to the water, dinting its top with sweat,
And see, before I can drink,

A startled inchling trout
Of spotted near-transparency,
Trawling a shadow solider than he.
He swerves now, darting out

To where, in a flicked slew
Of sparks and glittering silt, he weaves
Through stream-bed rocks, disturbing foundered leaves,
And butts then out of view

Beneath a sliding glass
Crazed by the skimming of a brace
Of burnished dragon-flies across its face,
In which deep cloudlets pass

And a white precipice
Of mirrored birch-trees plunges down
Toward where the azures of the zenith drown.
How shall I drink all this?

Joy's trick is to supply
Dry lips with what can cool and slake,
Leaving them dumbstruck also with an ache
Nothing can satisfy.

October 1982

I now wish that I had spent somewhat more of my life with verse. This is not because I fear having missed out on truths that are incapable of statement in prose. There are no such truths; there is nothing about death that Swinburne and Landor knew but Epicurus and Heidegger failed to grasp. Rather, it is because I would have lived more fully if I had been able to rattle off more old chestnuts—just as I would have if I had made more close friends. Cultures with richer vocabularies are more fully human—farther removed from the beasts—than those with poorer ones; individual men and women are more fully human when their memories are amply stocked with verses.

RICHARD RORTY, November 2007

Old Folk's Home, Jerusalem

For Harry Timar

Evening, the bees fled, the honeysuckle
in its golden dotage, all the sickrooms ajar.
Law of the Innocents: What doesn't end, sloshes over . . .
even here, where destiny girds the cucumber.

So you wrote a few poems. The horned
thumbnail hooked into an ear doesn't care.
The gray underwear wadded over a belt says So what.

The night air is minimalist,
a needlepoint with raw moon as signature.
In this desert the question's not
Can you see? but *How far off?*
Valley settlements put on their lights
like armor; there's finch chit and my sandal's
inconsequential crunch.

Everyone waiting here was once in love.

October 1985

DON PATERSON

The Lie

As was my custom, I'd risen a full hour
before the house had woken to make sure
that everything was in order with The Lie,
his drip changed and his shackles all secure.

I was by then so practiced in this chore
I'd counted maybe thirteen years or more
since last I'd felt the urge to meet his eye.
Such, I liked to think, was our rapport.

I was at full stretch to test some ligature
when I must have caught a ragged thread, and tore
his gag away; though as he made no cry,
I kept on with my checking as before.

Why do you call me The Lie? he said. I swore:
it was a child's voice. I looked up from the floor.
The dark had turned his eyes to milk and sky
and his arms and legs were all one scarlet sore.

He was a boy of maybe three or four.
His straps and chains were all the things he wore.
Knowing I could make him no reply
I took the gag before he could say more

and put it back as tight as it would tie
and locked the door and locked the door and locked the door

September 2009

MAXINE KUMIN

Nurture

From a documentary on marsupials I learn
that a pillowcase makes a fine
substitute pouch for an orphaned kangaroo.

I am drawn to such dramas of animal rescue.
They are warm in the throat. I suffer, the critic proclaims,
from an overabundance of maternal genes.

Bring me your fallen fledgling, your bummer lamb,

lead the abused, the starvelings, into my barn.
Advise the hunted deer to leap into my corn.

And had there been a wild child—
filthy and fierce as a ferret, he is called
in one nineteenth-century account—

a wild child to love, it is safe to assume,
given my fireside inked with paw prints,
there would have been room.

Think of the language we two, same and not-same,
might have constructed from sign,
scratch, grimace, grunt, vowel:

Laughter our first noun, and our long verb, howl.

October 1987

Paterson, Book V: *The River of Heaven*

Of asphodel, that greeny flower, the least,

       that is a simple flower

              like a buttercup upon its

branching stem, save

       that it's green and wooden

              We've had a long life

and many things have happened in it.

       There are flowers also

              in hell. So today I've come

to talk to you about them, among

       other things, of flowers

              that we both love, even

of this poor, colorless

       thing which no one living

              prizes but the dead see

and ask among themselves,

       What do we remember that was shaped

              as this thing

is shaped? while their eyes

      fill

                with tears. By which

and by the weak wash of crimson

          colors it, the rose

              is predicated

                    October 1952

TED HUGHES

Heatwave

Between Westminster and sunstruck St. Paul's
The desert has entered the flea's belly.

Like shut-eyed half-submerged Nile bulls
The buildings tremble with breath.

The mirage of river is so real
Bodies drift in it, and human rubbish.

The main thing is the silence.
There are no charts for the silence.

Men can't penetrate it. Till sundown
Releases its leopard

Over the roofs, and women are suddenly
Everywhere, and the walker's bones

Melt in the coughing of great cats.

December 1963

FRANK O'HARA

Chez Jane

The white chocolate jar full of petals
swills odds and ends around in a dizzying eye
of four o'clocks now and to come. The tiger,
marvellously striped and irritable, leaps
on the table and without disturbing a hair
of the flowers' breathless attention, pisses
into the pot, right down its delicate spout.
A whisper of steam goes up from that porcelain
urethra. "Saint-Saëns!" it seems to be whispering,
curling unerringly around the furry nuts
of the terrible puss, who is mentally flexing.
Ah be with me always, spirit of noisy
contemplation in the studio, the Garden
of Zoos, the eternally fixed afternoons!
There, while music scratches its scrofulous
stomach, the brute beast emerges and stands,
clear and careful, knowing always the exact peril
at this moment caressing his fangs with
a tongue given wholly to luxurious usages;
which only a moment before dropped aspirin
in this sunset of roses, and now throws a chair
in the air to aggravate the truly menacing.

November 1954

The most whimsical work is the result of seriousness and nothing else. Any man who does not take his technique—which means saying what he means and not saying what he does not mean—with bitter seriousness, is a jackass. The sign of a poet's unforgiving seriousness is his rebellious laughter, which he guards with immaculate craft.

WILLIAM CARLOS WILLIAMS, July 1919

An isolation from the audience *by poetry* is a fairly gratifying situation, for inside each poet, I suspect, lurks a Garboesque desire.

FRANK O'HARA, February 1957

REGINALD DWAYNE BETTS

"For you: anthophilous, lover of flowers"

For you: anthophilous, lover of flowers,
green roses, chrysanthemums, lilies: retrophilia,
philocaly, philomath, sarcophilous—all this love,
of the past, of beauty, of knowledge, of flesh; this is
catalogue & counter: philalethist, negrophile, neophile.
A negro man walks down the street, taps Newport
out against a brick wall & stares at you. Love
that: lygophilia, lithophilous. Be amongst stones,
amongst darkness. We are glass house. Philopornist,
philotechnical. Why not worship the demimonde?
Love that—a corner room, whatever is not there,
all the clutter you keep secret. Palaeophile,
ornithophilous: you, antiquarian, pollinated by birds.
All this a way to dream green rose petals on the bed you love;
petrophilous, stigmatophilia: live near rocks, tattoo hurt;
for you topophilia: what place do you love? All these words
for love (for you), all these ways to say believe
in symphily, to say let us live near each other.

September 2011

RACHEL WETZSTEON

On Leaving the Bachelorette Brunch

Because I gazed out the window at birds
doing backflips when the subject turned
to diamonds, because my eyes glazed over
with the slightly sleepy sheen your cake will wear,

never let it be said that I'd rather be
firing arrows at heart-shaped dartboards
or in a cave composing polyglot puns.
I crave, I long for transforming love

as surely as leaves need water and mouths seek bread.
But I also fear the colder changes
that lie in wait and threaten to turn
moons of honey to pools of molasses,

broad front porches to narrow back gardens
and tight rings of friendship to flimsy things
that break when a gold band brightly implies
leave early, go home, become one with the one

the world has told you to tend and treasure
above all others. You love, and that's good;
you are loved, that's superb; you will vanish
and reap some happy rewards. But look at the birds.

November 2004

ADRIAN BLEVINS

How to Cook a Wolf

If your mother's like mine wanting you honeyed and blithe
    you'll get cooked by getting evicted

since the mothers can teach with a dustpan the tons of modes of
    tossing.

And the fathers will lift your eyes too-early-too-open:
    the fathers can creep up on anything when it's still too wet

to cloister with their weeping and strand you like a seed

or cook at the carnivals with the can-do caroling
    and storefronts and foodstuffs and annulments and Scotch

and off-handed fucking and walking out and moving on

until they're cooking the drift of you wanting a whole bayou up in
    you
        and cooking and cooking the gist

of you needing your crannies hot with a good man's body-silt

until your head is stuffed with a pining for diapers
    and the most minuscule spoons made mostly of silver

and Ajax too and Minwax Oh

in this the dumbstruck story of the American female
    as a cut of terracotta and some kindling in a dress

while howling at the marrow of the marrow of the bone.

October 2008

Gravelly Run

I don't know somehow it seems sufficient
to see and hear whatever coming and going is,
losing the self to the victory
    of stones and trees,
of bending sandpit lakes, crescent

round groves of dwarf pine:
for it is not so much to know the self
as to know it as it is known
    by galaxy and cedar cone,
as if birth had never found it

and death could never end it:
the swamp's slow water comes
down Gravelly Run fanning the long
    stone-held algal
hair and narrowing roils between

the shoulders of the highway bridge:
holly grows on the banks in the woods there,
and the cedars' gothic-clustered
    spires could make
green religion in winter bones: so I

look and reflect, but the air's glass
jail seals each thing in its entity:
no use to make any philosophies here:
    I see no
god in the holly, hear no song from

the snowbroken weeds: Hegel is not the winter
yellow in the pines: the sunlight has never
heard of trees: surrendered self among
    unwelcoming forms: stranger,
hoist your burdens, get on down the road.

November 1960

Possibly there is such a thing as being so concerned with the self that one loses sight of the poet's privileged duty, which is to be concerned with everything, in the hope of producing something—a poem, a stanza, even a single line—that will live on its own, in its own time.

CLIVE JAMES, July/August 2009

All human music has a dying fall.

SISTER BERNETTA QUINN, OSF, May 1971

SAMUEL MENASHE

Here

Ghost I house
In this old flat—
Your outpost—
My aftermath

April 2004

ROBERT DUNCAN

Returning to Roots of First Feeling

Feld, groes or *goers, hus, doeg, dung,*
in field, grass, house, day and dung we share
with those that in the forests went
    singers and dancers out of the dream;
for cradles, goods and hallows came
    long before Christendom,
wars and warblers-of-the-world where

me bifel a ferly, a fairy me thoughte:
and those early and those late saw
some of them poets
a faire felde ful of folke fonde I there bitwene,
for the vain and the humble go into one Man
and as best we can we make his song,

a simple like making of night and day
encumbered by vestiges and forebodings
in words of need and hope striving
to awaken the old keeper of the living
and restore lasting melodies of his desire.

October 1959

JACOB SAENZ

Sweeping the States

they move in swift on the Swift
Plants in six states & sift
through the faces to separate
the dark from the light

like meat & seat them in
the back of vans packed tight
like the product they pack
& who's to pick up the slack

the black & white can't cut it
so the beef stacks sell single
to feed the pack   the flock
who block passages & clog

the cogs of the machine   the process
not so swift to give & grant a wish
of a place   a stake in the land
handling the steaks for the rest

to take in   to sate the mouths
of the stock who have stock
in the business of beef & beef
with the brown who ground them

November 2007

Blues in Stereo

YOUR NUMBER'S COMING OUT!
BOUQUETS I'LL SEND YOU
AND DREAMS I'LL SEND YOU
AND HORSES SHOD WITH GOLD
ON WHICH TO RIDE IF MOTOR CARS
WOULD BE TOO TAME—
TRIUMPHAL ENTRY SEND YOU—
SHOUTS FROM THE EARTH ITSELF
BARE FEET TO BEAT THE GREAT DRUM BEAT
OF GLORY TO YOUR NAME AND MINE—
ONE AND THE SAME:
YOU BAREFOOT, TOO,
IN THE QUARTER OF THE NEGROES
WHERE AN ANCIENT RIVER FLOWS
PAST HUTS THAT HOUSE A MILLION BLACKS
AND THE WHITE GOD NEVER GOES
FOR THE MOON WOULD WHITE HIS WHITENESS
BEYOND ITS MASK OF WHITENESS
AND THE NIGHT MIGHT BE ASTONISHED
AND SO LOSE ITS REPOSE.

IN A TOWN NAMED AFTER STANLEY
NIGHT EACH NIGHT COMES NIGHTLY

AND THE MUSIC OF OLD MUSIC'S
BORROWED FOR THE HORNS
THAT DON'T KNOW HOW TO PLAY
ON LPs THAT WONDER
HOW THEY EVER GOT THAT WAY.

African
drums
beat
over
blues
that
gradually

> WHAT TIME IS IT, MAMA?
> WHAT TIME IS IT NOW?
> MAKES NO DIFFERENCE TO ME—
> BUT I'M ASKING ANYHOW.
> WHAT TIME IS IT, MAMA?
> WHAT TIME NOW?

mount
in
intensity
to
end
in
climax.

DOWN THE LONG HARD ROW THAT I BEEN
   HOEING
I THOUGHT I HEARD THE HORN OF PLENTY
   BLOWING
BUT I GOT TO GET A NEW ANTENNA, LORD—
MY TV KEEPS ON SNOWING.

Then

silence.

August 1961

JAMES SCHUYLER

Korean Mums

beside me in this garden
are huge and daisy-like
(why not? are not
oxeye daisies a chrysanthemum?),
shrubby and thick-stalked,
the leaves pointing up
the stems from which
the flowers burst in
sunbursts. I love
this garden in all its moods,
even under its winter coat
of salt hay, or now,
in October, more than
half gone over: here
a rose, there a clump
of aconite. This morning
one of the dogs killed
a barn owl. Bob saw
it happen, tried to
intervene. The airedale
snapped its neck and left
it lying. Now the bird
lies buried by an apple
tree. Last evening
from the table we saw
the owl, huge in the dusk,
circling the field
on owl-silent wings.
The first one ever seen
here: now it's gone,
a dream you just remember.

The dogs are barking. In
the studio music plays
and Bob and Darragh paint.
I sit scribbling in a little
notebook at a garden table,
too hot in a heavy shirt
in the mid-October sun
into which the Korean mums
all face. There is a
dull book with me,
an apple core, cigarettes,
an ashtray. Behind me
the rue I gave Bob
flourishes. Light on leaves,
so much to see, and
all I really see is that
owl, its bulk troubling
the twilight. I'll
soon forget it: what
is there I have not forgot?
Or one day will forget:
this garden, the breeze
in stillness, even
the words, Korean mums.

February 1976

It seems to me that the central argument of American poetry is, and to a certain extent always has been, whether to accept or to reject America.

KARL SHAPIRO, February 1947

Birthplace: New Rochelle

Returning to that house
And the rounded rocks of childhood—   they have lasted well.

A world of things.

An aging man,
The knuckles of my hand
So jointed! I am this?

               The house
My father's once, and the ground. There is a color of
          his times
In the sun's light.

A generation's mark.
It intervenes. My child
No more a child, our child
Not altogether lone in a lone universe that suffers time
Like stones in sun. For we do not.

                          January 1960

GARY SNYDER

Song of the Tangle

Two thigh hills hold us at the fork
                round mount center

            we sit all folded
on the dusty planed planks of a shrine
drinking top class saké that was left
                for the god.

calm tree halls
the sun past the summit
heat sunk through the vines,
                twisted sasa

cicada singing,
                swirling in the tangle

the tangle of the thigh

            the brush
            through which we push

                            March 1968

A Child's Garden of Gods

The summer that my mother fell
Into the hole that was herself,
We children sat like china dolls
Waiting mutely on a shelf
    For the horror to be done.

My father, who'd begun to drink
Jasmine from a turquoise cup,
Was practicing his yoga when
That dark mood swallowed Mama up.
    His trance was not undone.

When autumn came, like birds on wire,
Tilting forward in our rows,
We waited for our father to
Rise from his oriental pose
    And save the fallen lady.

We stood around the stone-cold stove
The day her secrets gave her back.
She ran, and though her hair was damp,
And though her fingernails were black,
    Our mother still looked pretty.

She made a fire to thaw us out,
And after we were nicely browned,
She hugged us each, and told us all
About her travels underground.
    Her eyes were black as coffee.

She showed us bits of root and seed,
And other treasure found below:
Eye-tooth of mole, old human bone,
And jewels she'd hidden long ago.
    The buried always grow.

It's winter still. Our father sits
Cross-legged with an empty bowl.
Unmoved in the deserted yard,
He stares with perfect self-control
Into a wall of snow.

July 1961

ISABELLA GARDNER
The Widow's Yard

"Snails lead slow idyllic lives" . . .
The rose and the laurel leaves
in the raw young widow's yard
were littered with silver. Hard-
ly a leaf lacked the decimal scale
of the self of a snail. Frail
in friendship I observed with care
these creatures (meaning to spare
the widow's vulnerable eyes
the hurting pity in my gaze).

Snails, I said, are tender skinned.
Excess in nature . . . sun rain wind
are killers. To save themselves
snails shrink to shelter in their shells
where they wait safe and patient
until the elements are gent-
ler. And do they not have other foes?
the widow asked. Turtles crows
foxes rats, I replied, and canned
heat that picnickers aban-
don. Also parasites invade
their flesh and alien eggs are laid
inside their skins. Their mating
too is perilous. The meeting
turns their faces blue with bliss
and consummation of this
absolute embrace is so
extravagantly slow
in coming that love begun
at dawn may end in fatal sun.

The widow told me that her
husband knew snails' ways and his gar-
den had been Eden for them. He
said the timid snail could lift three
times his weight straight up and haul
a wagon toy loaded with a whole
two hundred times his body's burden.
Then as we left the garden
she said that at the first faint chill
the first premonition of fall
the snails go straight to earth . . . excrete
the lime with which they then secrete
the opening in their shells . . . and wait for spring.
It is those little doors which sing,
she said, when they are boiled.
She smiled at me when I recoiled.

September 1957

THOM GUNN

Lines for a Book

I think of all the toughs through history
And thank heaven they lived, continually.
Their pride exalted some, some overthrew,
But was not vanity at last: they knew
That though the mind has also got a place
It's not in marvelling at its mirrored face
And evident sensibility. It's better
To go and see your friend than write a letter;
To be a soldier than to be a cripple;
To take an early weaning from the nipple
Than think your mother is the only girl;
To be insensitive, to steel the will,
Than sit irresolute all day at stool
Inside the heart; and to despise the fool,
Who may not help himself and may not choose,
Than give him pity which he cannot use.
I think of those exclusive by their action,
For whom mere thought could be no satisfaction—
The athletes lying under tons of dirt
Or standing gelded so they cannot hurt
The pale curators and the families
By calling up disturbing images.
I think of all the toughs through history
And thank heaven they lived, continually.

June 1955

"I, too, dislike it," are the immortal beginning words of Marianne Moore's poem "Poetry," and they seem to me to be the only possible credentials for a poet and a reader of poetry. I sometimes wonder if there are any poets who "like" it, and whether I would like them.

MICHAEL HOFMANN, September 2005

From "The Third Hour of the Night"

Understand that it can drink till it is
sick, but cannot drink till it is satisfied.

It alone knows you. It does not wish you well.

Understand that when your mother, in her only
pregnancy, gave birth to twins

painfully stitched into the flesh, the bone of one child

was the impossible-to-remove cloak that confers
invisibility. The cloak that maimed it gave it power.

Painfully stitched into the flesh, the bone of the other child

was the impossible-to-remove cloak that confers
visibility. The cloak that maimed it gave it power.

Envying the other, of course each twin

tried to punish and become the other.
Understand that when the beast within you

succeeds again in paralyzing into unending

incompletion whatever you again had the temerity to
try to make

its triumph is made sweeter by confirmation of its

rectitude. It knows that it alone
knows you. It alone remembers your mother's

mother's grasping immigrant bewildered

stroke-filled slide-to-the-grave
you wiped from your adolescent American feet.

Your hick purer-than-thou overreaching veiling

mediocrity. Understand that you can delude others but
not what you more and more

now call the beast within you. Understand

the cloak that maimed each gave each power.
Understand that there is a beast within you

that can drink till it is

sick, but cannot drink till it is satisfied. Understand
that it will use the conventions of the visible world

to turn your tongue to stone. It alone

knows you. It does
not wish you well. *These are instructions for the wrangler.*

October 2004

WILLIAM MEREDITH

The Illiterate

Touching your goodness, I am like a man
Who turns a letter over in his hand,
And you might think this was because the hand
Was unfamiliar, but truth is the man
Has never had a letter from anyone;
And now he is both afraid of what it means
And ashamed because he has no other means
To find out what it says than to ask someone.

His uncle could have left the store to him,
Or his parents died before he sent them word,
Or the dark girl changed and want him for her lover.
Afraid and letter-proud he keeps it with him.
What would you call his pleasure in the words
That keep him rich and orphaned and beloved?

August 1953

RHINA P. ESPAILLAT

Changeling

I want to tell myself she is not you,
this sullen woman wearing Mama's eyes
all wrong, whose every gesture rings untrue
and yet familiar. In your harsh disguise
I sometimes need to find you, sometimes fear
I will, if I look closely into her.
I want to tell myself you are not here,
trapped in this parody of what you were,
but love was never safe: it lives on danger,
finds what can't be found by any other
power on Earth or over it. This stranger
is you, is all the you there is, my mother
whose gentler face is gone beyond recall,
and I must love you so, or not at all.

August 1991

MARIA HUMMEL

Station

Days you are sick, we get dressed slow,
find our hats, and ride the train.
We pass a junkyard and the bay,
then a dark tunnel, then a dark tunnel.

You lose your hat. I find it. The train
sighs open at Burlingame,
past dark tons of scrap and water.
I carry you down the black steps.

Burlingame is the size of joy:
a race past bakeries, gold rings
in open black cases. I don't care
who sees my crooked smile

or what erases it, past the bakery,
when you tire. We ride the blades again
beside the crooked bay. You smile.
I hold you like a hole holds light.

We wear our hats and ride the knives.
They cannot fix you. They try and try.
Tunnel! Into the dark open we go.
Days you are sick, we get dressed slow.

September 2010

JAMES MERRILL

The Mad Scene

Again last night I dreamed the dream called Laundry.
In it, the sheets and towels of a life we were going to share,
The milk-stiff bibs, the shroud, each rag to be ever
Trampled or soiled, bled on or groped for blindly,
Came swooning out of an enormous willow hamper
Onto moon-marbly boards. We had just met. I watched
From outer darkness. I had dressed myself in clothes
Of a new fiber that never stains or wrinkles, never
Wears thin. The opera house sparkled with tiers
And tiers of eyes, like mine enlarged by belladonna,
Trained inward. There I saw the cloud-clot, gust by gust,
Form, and the lightning bite, and the roan mane unloosen.
Fingers were running in panic over the flute's nine gates.
Why did I flinch? I loved you. And in the downpour laughed
To see us wrung white, gnarled together, one
Topmost mordent of wisteria,
As the lean tree burst into grief.

October 1962

The deeper register of your understanding, which includes that sense that "we're going to have to pay for it," has to be there somehow—even in a celebratory poem. The grieving register is one that better not be shut off: it surely is something poetry has to take cognizance of.

SEAMUS HEANEY, December 2008

It is worthy of remark that poetry needs no defense, is its own reason for being, and, having been defended for centuries, is still defenseless and most bright where most naked.

RICHARD EBERHART, November 1950

W. S. GRAHAM

The Beast in the Space

Shut up. Shut up. There's nobody here.
If you think you hear somebody knocking
On the other side of the words, pay
No attention. It will be only
The great creature that thumps its tail
On silence on the other side.
If you do not even hear that
I'll give the beast a quick skelp
And through Art you'll hear it yelp.

The beast that lives on silence takes
Its bite out of either side.
It pads and sniffs between us. Now
It comes up and laps my meaning up.
Call it over. Call it across
This curious, necessary space.
Get off, you terrible inhabiter
Of silence. I'll not have it. Get
Away to whoever it is will have you.

He's gone and if he's gone to you
That's fair enough. For on this side
Of the words it's late. The heavy moth
Bangs on the pane. The whole house
Is sleeping and I remember
I am not here, only the space
I sent the terrible beast across.
Watch. He bites. Listen gently
To any song he snorts or growls
And give him food. He means neither
Well or ill towards you. Above
All, shut up. Give him your love.

April 1967

WILLIAM BUTLER YEATS

The Fisherman

Although I can see him still—
The freckled man who goes
To a gray place on a hill
In gray Connemara clothes
At dawn to cast his flies—
It's long since I began
To call up to the eyes
This wise and simple man.
All day I'd looked in the face
What I had hoped it would be
To write for my own race
And the reality:
The living men that I hate,
The dead man that I loved,
The craven man in his seat,
The insolent unreproved—
And no knave brought to book
Who has won a drunken cheer—
The witty man and his joke
Aimed at the commonest ear,
The clever man who cries
The catch cries of the clown,
The beating down of the wise
And great Art beaten down.

Maybe a twelve-month since
Suddenly I began,
In scorn of this audience,
Imagining a man,

And his sun-freckled face
And gray Connemara cloth,
Climbing up to a place
Where stone is dark with froth,
And the down turn of his wrist
When the flies drop in the stream—
A man who does not exist,
A man who is but a dream;
And cried, "Before I am old
I shall have written him one
Poem maybe as cold
And passionate as the dawn."

February 1916

The artist is not dependent upon the multitude of his listeners. Humanity is the rich effluvium, it is the waste and the manure and the soil, and from it grows the tree of the arts. As the plant germ seizes upon the noble particles of the earth, upon the light-seeking and the intrepid, so does the artist seize upon those souls which do not fear transfusion and transmutation, which dare become the body of the god . . .

It is true that the great artist has always a great audience, even in his life time; but it is not the *vulgo* but the spirits of irony and of destiny and of humor, sitting within him.

EZRA POUND, October 1914

No small group today can suffice for the poet's immediate audience, as such groups did in the stay-at-home aristocratic ages; and the greatest danger which besets modern art is that of slighting the "great audience" whose response alone can give it authority and volume, and of magnifying the importance of a coterie.

HARRIET MONROE, October 1914 (responding to Pound)

Acknowledgments

We would like to thank Stephanie Hlywak for cheerfully keeping us on track through each stage of this book's preparation, James Sitar and Michael Slosek for their patient and diligent permissions work, Michael Robbins for researching and compiling the contributors' notes, and above all Valerie Jean Johnson, Fred Sasaki, and Lindsay Garbutt of the *Poetry* magazine staff for essential support of many kinds. We are also grateful to the following at the University of Chicago Press: Alan Thomas for his invaluable and attentive editorial guidance, Randy Petilos, Isaac Tobin for his bold book design, Kelly Finefrock-Creed for copyediting, and publicist Levi Stahl.

A. R. AMMONS: "Gravelly Run" from *Collected Poems 1951–1971* by A. R. Ammons. Copyright © 1960 by A. R. Ammons. Used by permission of the estate and W.W. Norton & Company, Inc.

MARGARET ATWOOD: "Songs of the Transformed" from *Selected Poems 1965–1975* by Margaret Atwood. Copyright © 1976 by Margaret Atwood. Reprinted by permission of Houghton Mifflin Harcourt Publishing Company. All rights reserved. "Pig Song" by Margaret Atwood. Available in the following collections: in the United States, *Selected Poems II: 1965–1975*, published by Houghton Mifflin, copyright © 1976 by Margaret Atwood; in Canada, *Selected Poems 1966–1984*, copyright © 1990 by Oxford University Press Canada, reprinted by permission of the publisher; in the United Kingdom, *Eating Fire*, published by Virago Books, copyright © 1998 by Margaret Atwood. Used by permission of the author.

W. H. AUDEN: "The Shield of Achilles" copyright © 1952 by W. H. Auden. Reprinted by permission of Curtis Brown, Ltd.

AMIRI BARAKA: "Valéry as Dictator" reprinted by permission of SLL/Sterling Lord Literistic, Inc. Copyright © by Amiri Baraka.

JOHN BERRYMAN: "The Traveller" from *Collected Poems: 1937–1971* by John Berryman. Copyright © 1989 by Kate Donahue Berryman. Reprinted by permission of Farrar, Straus and Giroux, LLC, and by Faber & Faber, Ltd.

LOUISE BOGAN: "Night" from *The Blue Estuaries* by Louise Bogan. Copyright © 1968 by Louise Bogan. Copyright © renewed 1996 by Ruth Limmer. Reprinted by permission of Farrar, Straus and Giroux, LLC.

GWENDOLYN BROOKS: "The Children of the Poor" from *Blacks* (1991). Reprinted by consent of Brooks Permissions.

BASIL BUNTING: Excerpt from "Briggflatts" from *Complete Poems*, edited by Richard Caddel (Bloodaxe Books, 2000). Reprinted by permission of Bloodaxe Books.

CID CORMAN: Excerpt from "Cahoots" used by permission of Bob Arnold, literary executor for the Estate of Cid Corman.

HART CRANE: "At Melville's Tomb" from *Complete Poems of Hart Crane* by Hart Crane, edited by Marc Simon. Copyright © 1933, 1958, 1966 by Liveright Publishing Corporation. Copyright © 1986 by Marc Simon. Used by permission of Liveright Publishing Corporation.

ROBERT CREELEY: "For Love" from *Collected Poems 1945–1975*, published in 2006. Used by permission of the University of California Press.

E. E. CUMMINGS: "What If a Much of a Which of a Wind" from *Complete Poems: 1904–1962* by E. E. Cummings, edited by George J. Firmage. Copyright © 1944, 1972, 1991 by the Trustees for the E. E. Cummings Trust. Used by permission of Liveright Publishing Corporation.

H. D.: "Delphi" (excerpt of "His Presence") by H. D. (Hilda Doolittle) from *Collected Poems, 1912–1944*. Copyright © 1982 by the Estate of Hilda Doolittle. Reprinted by permission of New Directions Publishing Corp. and Carcanet Press Limited.

TOM DISCH: "The Prisoners of War" published originally in the September 1972 issue of *Poetry* magazine. All rights reserved by the Estate of Thomas M. Disch c/o Writers Representatives LLC, New York, NY 10011.

EDWARD DORN: "Dark Ceiling" from *Geography* (Fulcrum Press, 1965). Used by permission.

RITA DOVE: "Old Folk's Home, Jerusalem" from *Grace Notes* by Rita Dove. Copyright © 1989 by Rita Dove. Used by permission of the author and W.W. Norton & Company, Inc.

ALAN DUGAN: "Fabrication of Ancestors" from *Poems Seven: New and Complete Poetry*. Copyright © 2001 by Alan Dugan. Reprinted with the permission of the Permissions Company, Inc., on behalf of Seven Stories Press (www.sevenstories .com).

ROBERT DUNCAN: "Returning to Roots of First Feeling" from *The Opening of the Field* by Robert Duncan. Copyright © 1960 by Robert Duncan. Reprinted by permission of New Directions Publishing Corp.

RHINA P. ESPAILLAT: "Changeling" from *Lapsing to Grace* by Rhina P. Espaillat. Copyright © 1992 by Rhina P. Espaillat. Reprinted by permission of the author.

ALICE FULTON: "What I Like" from *Dance Script with Electric Ballerina: Poems*. Copyright © 1983 by Alice Fulton. Used with permission of the poet and the University of Illinois Press.

ISABELLA GARDNER: "The Widow's Yard" from *The Collected Poems*. Copyright © 1990 by the Estate of Isabella Gardner. Reprinted with the permission of the Permissions Company, Inc., on behalf of BOA Editions, Ltd. (www.boaeditions.org).

W. S. GRAHAM: "The Beast in the Space" from *Collected Poems 1942–1977* by W. S. Graham. Copyright © by the Estate of W. S. Graham. Used by permission.

THOM GUNN: "Lines for a Book" from *Collected Poems* by Thom Gunn. Copyright © 1994 by Thom Gunn. Reprinted by permission of Farrar, Straus and Giroux, LLC, and by Faber & Faber, Ltd.

MICHAEL S. HARPER: "Blues Alabama" from *Songlines in Michaeltree: New and Collected Poems*. Copyright © 2000 by Michael S. Harper. Used with permission of the poet and the University of Illinois Press.

ROBERT HAYDEN: "O Daedalus, Fly Away Home" from *Collected Poems of Robert Hayden* by Robert Hayden, edited by Frederick Glaysher. Copyright © 1966 by Robert Hayden. Used by permission of Liveright Publishing Corporation.

LANGSTON HUGHES: "Blues in Stereo" from *The Collected Poems of Langston Hughes* by Langston Hughes, edited by Arnold Rampersad with David Roessel, associate editor. Copyright © 1994 by the Estate of Langston Hughes. Used by permission of Alfred A. Knopf, a division of Random House, Inc., and by Harold Ober Associates Incorporated.

TED HUGHES: "Heatwave" from *Collected Poems* by Ted Hughes. Copyright © 2003 by the Estate of Ted Hughes. Reprinted by permission of Farrar, Straus and Giroux, LLC, and by Faber & Faber, Ltd.

RANDALL JARRELL: "Protocols" from *The Complete Poems* by Randall Jarrell. Copyright © 1969, renewed 1997 by Mary von S. Jarrell. Reprinted by permission of Farrar, Straus and Giroux, LLC, and by Faber & Faber, Ltd.

ROBINSON JEFFERS: "The Trumpet, V. Grass on the Cliff," also published as "The Broken Balance, I. Reference to a Passage in Plutarch's Life of Sulla," in *The Collected Poetry of Robinson Jeffers, Volume 1*, edited by Tim Hunt. Copyright © 1938, renewed 1966 by Donnan and Garth Jeffers, Jeffers Literary Properties. All rights reserved. Used with permission of Stanford University Press (www.sup.org).

DONALD JUSTICE: "Men at Forty" from *Collected Poems of Donald Justice* by Donald Justice. Copyright © 2004 by Donald Justice. Used by permission of Alfred A. Knopf, a division of Random House, Inc.

WELDON KEES: "IV (Part of 'Eight Variations')" reprinted from *The Collected Poems of Weldon Kees*, edited by Donald Justice. Copyright © 1962, 1975 by the University of Nebraska Press. Copyright © renewed 2003 by the University of Nebraska Press. Used by permission of the University of Nebraska Press.

MAXINE KUMIN: "Nurture" from *Selected Poems 1960–1990* by Maxine Kumin. Copyright © 1989, 1997 by Maxine Kumin. Used by permission of the author and W. W. Norton & Company, Inc.

DENISE LEVERTOV: "Our Bodies" from *Poems 1960–1967* by Denise Levertov. Copyright © 1966 by Denise Levertov. Reprinted by permission of New Directions Publishing Corp.

WILLIAM MATTHEWS: "Mingus at the Showplace" from *Search Party: Collected Poems of William Matthews*. Copyright © 2004 by Sebastian Matthews and Stanley Plumly. All rights reserved. Reprinted by permission of Houghton Mifflin Harcourt Publishing Company.

WILLIAM MEREDITH: "The Illiterate" from *Effort at Speech: New and Selected Poems* by William Meredith, published by TriQuarterly Books / Northwestern University Press in 1997. Copyright © 1997 by William Meredith. All rights reserved. Used by permission of Northwestern University Press and Richard Harteis.

JAMES MERRILL: "The Mad Scene" from *Collected Poems* by James Merrill, edited by J. D. McClatchy and Stephen Yenser. Copyright © 2001 by the Literary Estate of James Merrill at Washington University. Used by permission of Alfred A. Knopf, a division of Random House, Inc.

W. S. MERWIN: "Search Party" from *Travels* by W. S. Merwin. Copyright © 1992 by W. S. Merwin. Used by permission of Alfred A. Knopf, a division of Random House, Inc. Also from *Selected Poems* (Blookaxe Books, 2007). Used by permission of Bloodaxe Books. Also used by permission of the Wylie Agency, LLC.

JOSEPHINE MILES: "The Hampton Institute Album," also published as "Down from Another Planet They Have Settled to Mend," by Josephine Miles from *A Kind of Affection* (Wesleyan University Press, 1967). Copyright © 1967 by Josephine Miles. Reprinted by permission of Wesleyan University Press.

EDNA ST. VINCENT MILLAY: "Rendezvous" copyright © 1939 by Edna St. Vincent Millay. Reprinted with permission of Holly Peppe, Literary Executor, The Millay Society.

MARIANNE MOORE: "No Swan So Fine," published in *The Poems of Marianne Moore*, edited by Grace Schulman (New York: Penguin, 2005). Permission for use herein is granted by the Literary Estate of Marianne C. Moore, David M. Moore, administrator of the Literary Estate of Marianne Moore. All rights reserved.

LISEL MUELLER: "In the Thriving Season" reprinted by permission of Louisiana State University Press.

LORINE NIEDECKER: "Three Poems" from *Collected Works*, published in 2004. Used by permission of the University of California Press.

FRANK O'HARA: "Chez Jane" from *Meditations in an Emergency*. Copyright © 1957 by Frank O'Hara. Used by permission of Grove/Atlantic, Inc.

GEORGE OPPEN: "Birthplace: New Rochelle" from *New Collected Poems* by George Oppen. Copyright © 1962 by George Oppen. Reprinted by permission of New Directions Publishing Corp. and Carcanet Press Limited.

P. K. PAGE: "My Chosen Landscape" from *The Hidden Room* (in two volumes) by P. K. Page. Copyright © 1997 by the Estate of P. K. Page. Reprinted by permission of the Porcupine's Quill.

SYLVIA PLATH: "Fever 103°" from *Ariel* by Sylvia Plath. Copyright © 1963 by Ted Hughes. Reprinted by permission of HarperCollins Publishers and by Faber & Faber, Ltd.

MARIE PONSOT: "Anti-Romantic" from *Admit Impediment* by Marie Ponsot. Copyright © 1958, 1960, 1964, 1977, 1979, 1980, 1981 by Marie Ponsot. Used by permission of Alfred A. Knopf, a division of Random House, Inc.

BELLE RANDALL: "A Child's Garden of Gods" from *101 Different Ways of Playing Solitaire and Other Poems* by Belle Randall. Copyright © 1973. Reprinted by permission of the University of Pittsburgh Press.

ADRIENNE RICH: "Final Notations" from *The Fact of a Doorframe: Selected Poems 1950–2001* by Adrienne Rich. Copyright © 1991, 2002 by Adrienne Rich. Used by permission of the author and W. W. Norton & Company, Inc.

THEODORE ROETHKE: "Root Cellar" from *Collected Poems of Theodore Roethke* by Theodore Roethke. Copyright © 1943 by Modern Poetry Association, Inc. Used by permission of Doubleday, a division of Random House, Inc., and Faber & Faber, Ltd.

MURIEL RUKEYSER: "Song." Copyright © 2006 by Muriel Rukeyser. Used by permission.

JAMES SCHUYLER: "Korean Mums" from *Collected Poems* by James Schuyler. Copyright © 1993 by the Estate of James Schuyler. Reprinted by permission of Farrar, Straus and Giroux, LLC.

DELMORE SCHWARTZ: "In the Naked Bed, In Plato's Cave" from *Selected Poems* by Delmore Schwartz. Copyright © 1959 by Delmore Schwartz. Reprinted by permission of New Directions Publishing Corp.

GARY SNYDER: "Song of the Tangle" from *Regarding Wave* by Gary Snyder. Copyright © 1970 by Gary Snyder. Reprinted by permission of New Directions Publishing Corp.

GEORGE STARBUCK: "Of Late" from *The Works: Poems Selected from Five Decades.* Copyright © 2003 by the University of Alabama Press. Used by permission.

RUTH STONE: "Forecast" used by permission of the author.

MAY SWENSON: "Green Red Brown and White" reprinted with permission of the Literary Estate of May Swenson. All rights reserved.

RICHARD WILBUR: "Hamlen Brook" from *Collected Poems 1943–2004* by Richard Wilbur. Copyright © 2004 by Richard Wilbur. Reprinted by permission of Houghton Mifflin Harcourt Publishing Company. All rights reserved.

WILLIAM CARLOS WILLIAMS: "Paterson, Book V: The River of Heaven" from *The Collected Poems: Volume II, 1939–1962* by William Carlos Williams. Copyright © 1948, 1962 by William Carlos Williams. Reprinted by permission of New Directions Publishing Corp. and Carcanet Press Limited.

JAMES WRIGHT: "The Blessing" from *Above the River: The Complete Poems and Selected Prose* by James Wright (Wesleyan University Press, 1990). Copyright © 1990 by James Wright. Reprinted by permission of Wesleyan University Press.

Contributors

A. R. AMMONS (1926–2001) wrote his first poems while serving aboard a Navy destroyer during World War II. His many books include *Ommateum, with Doxology* (1955), *Corsons Inlet* (1965), *Tape for the Turn of the Year* (1965), *Sphere: The Form of a Motion* (1974), *Worldly Hopes* (1982), and *Glare* (1997). He won the National Book Award twice, for *Collected Poems 1951–1971* in 1973 and in 1993 for *Garbage*. *A Coast of Trees* (1981) won the National Book Critics Circle Award. He was also the recipient of the Wallace Stevens Award, the Bollingen Prize, the Robert Frost Medal, and the Ruth Lilly Prize. Ammons taught at Cornell University.

RAE ARMANTROUT (b. 1947) is one of the founding members of the West Coast group of Language poets. Her books include *Extremities* (1978), *Precedence* (1985), *Made to Seem* (1995), *Veil: New and Selected Poems* (2001), *Up to Speed* (2004), *Next Life* (2007), and *Money Shot* (2011). *Versed* (2009) won the National Book Critics Circle Award and the Pulitzer Prize. Armantrout, recipient of *Poetry*'s 2008 Frederick Bock Prize, is professor and director of the New Writing Series at the University of California–San Diego.

CRAIG ARNOLD (1967–2009) won the 1998 Yale Younger Poets Competition for *Shells*. His second and final book, *Made Flesh*, appeared in 2008. He was a recipient of the Joseph Brodsky Rome Prize Fellowship from the American Academy of Arts and Letters, the US-Japan Creative Artists Exchange Fellowship, the Alfred Hodder Fellowship from Princeton University, and the Bess Hokin Prize from *Poetry* magazine. An enthusiast of volcanoes, Arnold went missing on the volcanic island of Kuchinoerabujima, Japan, in 2009 and is presumed dead.

MARGARET ATWOOD (b. 1939) is a Canadian poet, novelist, essayist, short-story writer, and environmental activist. Atwood first came to public attention as a poet in the sixties with her collections *Double Persephone* (1961), winner of the E. J. Pratt Medal, and *The Circle Game* (1964), winner of a Governor General's award. Subsequent collections include *Morning in the Burned House* (1995), *Eating Fire: Selected Poems 1965–1995* (1998), and *The Door* (2007). Atwood's novels include *The Handmaid's Tale* (1985) and *The Blind*

Assassin (2000). She is the recipient of several literary awards, including the Booker Prize and the Arthur C. Clarke Award.

W. H. AUDEN (1907–1973) was a poet, playwright, and librettist born in York, England. His first book, *Poems*, was published in 1930 with the help of T. S. Eliot. Notable among his several subsequent collections are *Another Time* (1940), *The Collected Poetry* (1945), and *The Shield of Achilles*, which won the National Book Award in 1956. His play *The Age of Anxiety* (1947) received the Pulitzer Prize. *The Dyer's Hand*, a book of criticism, appeared in 1962. Awarding Auden the National Medal for Literature in 1967, the National Book Committee wrote that "his work, branded by the moral and ideological fires of our age, breathes with eloquence, perception and intellectual power."

JOHN BERRYMAN (1914–1972) is best known for *The Dream Songs*, an intensely personal sequence of 385 poems which brought him the Pulitzer Prize and National Book Award. Born John Smith, Berryman was twelve when his father shot himself outside the boy's window. His works include *Homage to Mistress Bradstreet* (1956), *77 Dream Songs* (1964), and *His Toy, His Dream, His Rest* (1968). Berryman taught at the University of Minnesota from 1955 until his death.

REGINALD DWAYNE BETTS (b. 1980) is author of the memoir *A Question of Freedom* (Avery, 2009) and the poetry collection *Shahid Reads His Own Palm* (Alice James Books, 2010). He is a 2010 Soros Justice Fellow and 2011 Radcliffe Fellow.

FRANK BIDART (b. 1939) is a professor at Wellesley College. His books include *Golden State* (1973), *The Sacrifice* (1983), *In the Western Night: Collected Poems 1965–1990* (1990), and *Star Dust* (2005). *Desire* (1997) received the Theodore Roethke Memorial Poetry Prize and the Bobbitt Prize for Poetry and was nominated for the Pulitzer Prize, the National Book Award, and the National Book Critics Circle Award. Bidart's *Music Like Dirt* (2002) is the only poetry chapbook ever nominated for the Pulitzer Prize.

ADRIAN BLEVINS (b. 1964) won the 2004 Kate Tufts Discovery Award for *The Brass Girl Brouhaha*. Blevins is also the recipient of a Rona Jaffe Writers' Foundation Award for poetry and the Lamar York Prize for Nonfiction. She teaches at Colby College in Waterville, Maine.

LOUISE BOGAN (1897–1970) was born in Maine, the daughter of a mill worker. In New York, she befriended Malcolm Cowley, William Carlos Williams, and Edmund Wilson. Her books included *Body of This Death* (1923), *The Sleeping Fury* (1937), and *Collected Poems 1923–1953*, which received the Bollingen Prize in 1955. Bogan reviewed poetry for *The New Yorker* for thirty-eight years.

GWENDOLYN BROOKS (1917–2000) was the first African American woman to be appointed poetry consultant to the Library of Congress. Her first book of poems, *A Street in Bronzeville*, was published in 1945. In 1950 her second book, *Annie Allen,* won *Poetry* magazine's Eunice Tietjens Prize and the Pulitzer Prize for poetry, the first given to an African American. *In the Mecca* (1968) was nominated for the National Book Award. Other books include *The Bean Eaters* (1960), *We Real Cool* (1966), *Aurora* (1972), *Black Love* (1981), and *Children Coming Home* (1991). Brooks was also the recipient of the Frost Medal, the Shelley Memorial Award, and an award from the American Academy of Arts and Letters. She taught creative writing at several colleges and universities, including Columbia College Chicago, Elmhurst College, Columbia University, and the University of Wisconsin–Madison.

CHARLES BUKOWSKI (1920–1994) was born in Germany and brought to the United States at the age of two. A cult hero, Bukowski wrote more than forty books of poetry and prose, including *Flower, Fist, and Bestial Wail* (1959), *It Catches My Heart in Its Hands* (1963), *The Days Run Away like Wild Horses over the Hills* (1969), *Love Is a Dog from Hell* (1977), and *The Last Night of the Earth Poems* (1992). He also wrote the screenplay for *Barfly* (1987), a movie based on his life and starring Mickey Rourke.

BASIL BUNTING (1900–1985), described as "the last minor master of the modernist mode" by Donald Hall, was a leader of the new British literary avant-garde. Raised a Quaker, Bunting served time in prison as a conscientious objector during World War I. He is best known for *Briggflatts: An Autobiography* (1966); other works include *First Book of Odes* (1965) and *What the Chairman Told Tom* (1967).

LUCILLE CLIFTON (1936–2010) was the first author to have two books of poetry chosen as finalists for the Pulitzer Prize at once: *Good Woman: Poems and a Memoir, 1969–1980* and *Next: New Poems* (both 1987). Her collection *Two-Headed Woman* (1980), also a Pulitzer nominee, won the Juniper Prize from the University of Massachusetts. She served as Maryland's poet laureate from 1974 until 1985 and won the National Book Award for *Blessing the Boats: New and Selected Poems, 1988–2000* (2000). Awarded the Ruth Lilly Prize in 2007, Clifton was the Distinguished Professor of Humanities at St. Mary's College of Maryland.

BROOKLYN COPELAND (b. 1984) lives just north of Indianapolis. She received a Ruth Lilly Fellowship from the Poetry Foundation and is the author of the chapbook *Laked, Fielded, Blanked* (2011). Her first full-length collection will appear from Shearsman Books in 2012.

CID CORMAN (1924–2004) was a poet, translator, and editor, most notably of the literary magazine *Origin*. His dozens of works include *A Thanksgiving Eclogue from Theocritus* (1954), *January* (1960), *Sun Rock Man* (1962), *Livingdying* (1970), *So* (1978), and *In Particular* (1986). The first two volumes of his poems, *Of* (1990), contain nearly 1,500 poems. Corman spent many years in Japan.

HART CRANE (1899–1932), a central figure of American Modernism, was born the son of a prosperous candy maker. He dropped out of high school and moved to New York City, promising his parents he would attend Columbia University (he didn't). *White Buildings* appeared in 1926; he spent the next several years writing the long poem *The Bridge*, which met with critical disdain when it was published in 1930. Troubled by alcoholism, Crane traveled to Mexico on a Guggenheim Fellowship in 1931. He leapt into the Gulf of Mexico from the steamship SS *Orizaba* on April 27, 1932. His body was never recovered.

ROBERT CREELEY (1926–2005), once known primarily for his association with the Black Mountain poets, is now widely recognized as one of the most important and influential American poets of the twentieth century. A prolific poet and novelist, Creeley wrote more than sixty books, including *Pieces* (1968), *A Day Book* (1972), *Hello* (1976), *Windows* (1990), *If I were writing this* (2003), and *On Earth: Last Poems and an Essay* (2006). For several decades a professor at the State University of New York at Buffalo, Creeley was awarded the Bollingen Prize in 1999.

E. E. CUMMINGS (1894–1962) was a prolific poet, playwright, and novelist. He published his first collection of poems, *Tulips and Chimneys*, in 1923. Several poems deleted from the manuscript by the publisher were printed in 1925 as *&*, so titled because Cummings had wanted to use the ampersand, rather than the word "and," in the title of his first book. Other books include *is 5* (1926), *W (ViVa)* (1931), *No Thanks* (1935), and *XAIPE: Seventy-One Poems* (1950). Cummings received the Shelley Memorial Award, *Poetry*'s Harriet Monroe Prize, and the Bollingen Prize.

AVERILL CURDY (b. 1961) earned an MFA at the University of Houston and a PhD at the University of Missouri. She is the coeditor of *The Longman Anthology of Poetry* (2006). She has won the Rona Jaffe Foundation Writing Award, a Pushcart Prize, and a Lannan Writing Residency Fellowship. Curdy lives in Chicago and teaches at Northwestern University.

H. D. (1886–1961), born Hilda Doolittle, spent her childhood in the close-knit Moravian community in which her mother's family had been influential since its founding in the eighteenth century by a small band of believers persecuted for their membership in the Unitas Fratrum, a mystical Protestant sect. She met Ezra Pound when she was fifteen and struck up a friendship that later included William Carlos Williams. Her first book of poems, *Sea Garden*, was published in 1916. Subsequent books include *Hymen* (1921), *Trilogy* (1946), and *Helen in Egypt* (1961). She received the Guarantors Prize, the Levinson Prize, and the Harriet Monroe Memorial Prize from *Poetry*. She won the Brandeis University Creative Arts Award for Poetry in 1959 and in 1960 the Award of Merit Medal for Poetry from the American Academy of Arts and Letters.

W. S. DI PIERO (b. 1945) is a poet, essayist, art critic, and translator. His works include *Country of Survivors* (1974), *The Only Dangerous Thing* (1984), *The Dog Star* (1990), *Skirts and Slacks* (2001), and *Chinese Apples: New and Selected Poems* (2007). He has won awards for three of his poetry translations: Giacomo Leopardi's *Pensieri*, Sandro Penna's *This Strange Joy*, and Leonardo Sinisgalli's *The Ellipse*. Di Piero teaches at Stanford University.

TOM DISCH (1940–2008) was a poet, science-fiction novelist, and theater critic. His books of poetry include *ABCDEFG HIJKLM NPOQRST UVWXYZ* (1981), *Yes, Let's: New and Selected Poetry* (1989), and *Dark Verses and Light* (1991). His most notable novels are *Camp Concentration* (1968) and *334* (1972). Disch was also a children's author and published two volumes of poetry criticism. He committed suicide in 2008.

EDWARD DORN (1929–1999) was associated with the Black Mountain school of poetry, named for Black Mountain College in North Carolina, where he studied under Charles Olson. He is most well known for his cowboy drug epic *Gunslinger* (1968–69), known universally as *Slinger*, but he wrote more than twenty books, including *The Newly Fallen* (1961), *From Gloucester Out* (1964), *The North Atlantic Turbine* (1967), and *Hello, La Jolla* (1978). His selected poems were published as *Way More West* in 2007. Dorn was a professor at the University of Colorado at Boulder.

RITA DOVE (b. 1952) became the youngest person and the second African American to be named US poet laureate in 1993. Her poetry collections include *The Yellow House on the Corner* (1980), *Grace Notes* (1989), *On the Bus with Rosa Parks* (1999), and *Sonata Mulattica* (2009). *Thomas and Beulah* (1986) was awarded the Pulitzer Prize. Dove is a professor at the University of Virginia.

ALAN DUGAN (1923–2003) published his first book, *Poems*, in the Yale Series of Younger Poets in 1961. It received both the National Book Award and the

Pulitzer Prize. Subsequent books include *Poems 2* (1963), *Poems 3* (1967), and *Poems 4* (1974). *Poems Seven: New and Complete Poetry* (2001) also received the National Book Award. Dugan directed the Fine Arts Work Center in Provincetown, Massachusetts.

ROBERT DUNCAN (1919–1988) was adopted into a family of devout Theosophists and went on to be associated with both Black Mountain College and the San Francisco Renaissance. *The Opening of the Field* was published in 1960. His many other works include *Roots and Branches* (1964), *Bending the Bow* (1968), and the two volumes of *Ground Work* (1984, 1987). The first volume of his collected writings, *The H.D. Book*, appeared in 2011.

T. S. ELIOT (1888–1965) helped to define modern poetry to such an extent that few would disagree with the critic Northrop Frye's assessment: "A thorough knowledge of Eliot is compulsory for anyone interested in contemporary literature." *The Waste Land* is perhaps the most famous poem of the twentieth century, while Eliot's critical principles, as set forth in *The Sacred Wood* and other volumes, provided the impetus for the New Criticism.

THOMAS SAYERS ELLIS (b. 1963) is the author of *The Maverick Room* (2005) and *Skin, Inc.* (2010). He lives in Brooklyn, New York, and teaches at Sarah Lawrence College and in the Lesley University low-residency creative writing program.

RHINA P. ESPAILLAT (b. 1932) was born in the Dominican Republic under the dictatorship of Rafael Trujillo. After her great-uncle opposed the regime, her family was exiled to the United States and settled in New York City. Espaillat has published eleven poetry collections, including *Lapsing to Grace* (1992), *Where Horizons Go* (1998), winner of the T. S. Eliot Prize, *Rehearsing Absence* (2001), recipient of the Richard Wilbur Award, and *Playing at Stillness* (2005).

ALICE FULTON (b. 1952) is the author of several books of poetry, including *Palladium* (1986), winner of the National Poetry Series, *Powers of Congress* (1990), *Sensual Math* (1995), and *Felt* (2001), which was awarded the Rebekah Johnson Bobbitt National Prize for Poetry by the Library of Congress. She received the Bess Hokin Award from *Poetry* and in 2011 the American Academy of Arts and Letters Literature Award. Fulton teaches at Cornell University.

ISABELLA GARDNER (1915–1981) was the niece and namesake of the art collector Isabella Stewart Gardner and a cousin of the poet Robert Lowell. She became an associate editor of *Poetry* in 1951. In 1955 she published her first book of poems, *Birthdays from the Ocean*. Her other books are *The Looking Glass* (1961), *West of Childhood* (1965), and *That Was Then* (1979), nominated for an American Book Award.

ALBERT GOLDBARTH (b. 1948) has twice been awarded the National Book Critics Circle Award, for *Heaven and Earth: A Cosmology* (1991) and *Saving Lives* (2001). Other books include *Opticks: A Poem in Seven Sections* (1974), *Original Light: New and Selected Poems 1973–1983* (1983), and *Budget Travel through Space and Time* (2005). In 2008 he was awarded the Mark Twain Poetry Award from the Poetry Foundation. Goldbarth has taught for many years at Wichita State University.

W. S. GRAHAM (1918–1986) was born to a working-class family in Scotland and grew up in Clydeside, where he worked as an engineer. Graham's first collection of poetry, *Cage without Grievance,* was published in 1942. *The White Threshold* (1949) was his first important book. It was followed by *The Nightfishing* (1955), *Malcolm Mooney's Land* (1970), and *Implements in Their Places* (1977).

THOM GUNN (1929–2004) was born in Gravesend, Kent. At first associated with the Movement for his debut collection, *Fighting Terms* (1954), he moved to the United States in 1954. From 1960 he made his home in San Francisco's Haight-Ashbury district. His other books include *My Sad Captains* (1961), *Moly* (1971), *Jack Straw's Castle* (1976), and *Boss Cupid* (2000). *The Man with the Night Sweats* (1992) led to Gunn's receiving the Lenore Marshall Poetry Prize. He was also the recipient of the David Cohen Prize, the Levinson Prize, the W. H. Smith Award, the PEN (Los Angeles) Prize for Poetry, the Sara Teasdale Prize, a Lila Wallace-*Reader's Digest* Award, and the Forward Prize.

MICHAEL S. HARPER (b. 1938) was born in Brooklyn, New York. *Dear John, Dear Coltrane* appeared in 1970. *History is Your Own Heartbeat* (1971) won the Poetry Award of the Black Academy of Letters. Other collections include *Debridement* (1973), *Honorable Amendments* (1995), and *Songlines in Michaeltree: New and Collected Poems* (2000). Harper has been a professor at Brown University since 1970.

ROBERT HAYDEN (1913–1980) was born Asa Bundy Sheffey and raised by foster parents. His poetry collections include *Heart-Shape in the Dust* (1940) and *A Ballad of Remembrance* (1962), which was awarded the grand prize for poetry at the First World Festival of Negro Arts in Dakar, Senegal. He spent twenty-three years as a professor at Fisk University and ended his career with an eleven-year stint at the University of Michigan. In 1976 he became the first African American to be appointed as consultant in poetry to the Library of Congress (later known as poet laureate).

SEAMUS HEANEY (b. 1939) was born and raised in Castledawson, County Derry, Northern Ireland, and studied English at Queen's University of Belfast. His many books of poetry include *Death of a Naturalist* (1966), *Door into the Dark* (1969), *Wintering Out* (1972), *Field Work* (1979), *Station Island* (1984), *Seeing Things* (1991), and *District and Circle* (2006). He has won several awards, including the Geoffrey Faber Prize, the Whitbread Book of the Year Award, the David Cohen Prize, the Forward Prize, and the T. S. Eliot Prize. Heaney has taught at Queen's University, the University of California at Berkeley, and Harvard University. In 1995 he was awarded the Nobel Prize in Literature.

GEOFFREY HILL (b. 1932) was born into a working-class family in Worcestershire, England. His first book of poems, *For the Unfallen*, was published in 1959. Subsequent books include *King Log* (1968), *Mercian Hymns* (winner of the Alice Hunt Bartlett Prize, 1971), and *Tenebrae* (1978). After Hill moved to Boston in 1988 to teach at Boston University, he began to produce books at an accelerated rate. His late works include *The Triumph of Love* (1998), *Speech! Speech!* (2000), *The Orchards of Syon* (2002), *Without Title* (2006), and *A Treatise of Civil Power* (2007). Hill's *Selected Poems* was published in 2006. In 2009 his *Collected Critical Writings* won the Truman Capote Award for Literary Criticism. In 2010 he was elected Professor of Poetry at Oxford University.

LANGSTON HUGHES (1902–1967) was the leading figure of the Harlem Renaissance. His first book of poetry, *The Weary Blues*, was published in 1926. Other books include *Fine Clothes to the Jew* (1927), *The Dream Keeper and Other Poems* (1932), *Let America Be America Again* (1938), *Shakespeare in Harlem* (1942), and *Montage of a Dream Deferred* (1951). In 1960 the NAACP awarded Hughes the Spingarn Medal. In 1961 he was inducted into National Institute of Arts and Letters. In addition to his poetry, Hughes wrote plays, novels, and children's books.

TED HUGHES (1930–1998) was born in Mytholmroyd, in the West Riding district of Yorkshire. In 1956 he married Sylvia Plath, who encouraged him to submit his first manuscript, *The Hawk in the Rain*, to the Poetry Center's First Publication contest. The judges—Marianne Moore, W. H. Auden, and Stephen Spender—awarded it first prize. His several subsequent books of poetry include *Crow* (1971), *Cave Birds* (1979), *Moortown* (1980), *Selected Poems 1957–1981* (1982), *Flowers and Insects* (1986), and *Wolfwatching* (1990). He was also the author of several plays and children's books, including *The Iron Giant* (1968).

MARIA HUMMEL (b. 1973) is the author of the novel *Wilderness Run* (2002). She is a lecturer at Stanford University.

RODNEY JACK (1964–2008) served in the United States Navy for six years, and on board the USS *Missouri* during Operation Desert Storm. He received an MFA from Warren Wilson College, where he was a Holden Minority Fellow. He was also a GE Foundation Resident Artist of Color at Yaddo and a Bread Loaf Scholar. His work appeared in *AGNI, Blackbird, Open City, Ploughshares,* and *Poetry,* which awarded him the Eunice Tietjens Memorial Prize. In the fall of 2007, he returned to Warren Wilson as the Beebe Teaching Fellow. He took his own life in 2008.

RANDALL JARRELL (1914–1965) was a poet and literary critic. His books of poetry include *Blood for a Stranger* (1942), *Little Friend, Little Friend* (1945), and *The Lost World* (1965). *The Woman at the Washington Zoo* (1960) won the National Book Award. Jarrell was also the most influential literary critic of his generation; *Poetry and the Age,* his first collection of critical essays, was published in 1953. He taught at the University of Texas at Austin, Sarah Lawrence College, and the Woman's College of the University of North Carolina. Jarrell was struck by a car and killed near Chapel Hill in 1965; his death is believed to have been a suicide.

ROBINSON JEFFERS (1887–1962) was trained by his father, a Presbyterian minister, in Greek and Latin; by the time he began college at fifteen, he knew six languages. Jeffers's first volume of verse, *Flagons and Apples,* appeared in 1912, but it was the 1924 publication of *Tamar and Other Poems* that brought him attention. Other works include *The Double Axe* (1948) and *Hungerfield and Other Poems* (1954).

LEROI JONES (b. 1934)—poet, playwright, musicologist, social critic— changed his name in 1967 to Amiri Baraka. In the fifties Jones was associated with Beat poets like Allen Ginsberg and Jack Kerouac; in the sixties, he moved to Harlem and became a Black Nationalist, later turning his attention to third-world liberation movements. His many works include the poetry collection *Black Magic* (1967) and the play *Dutchman,* which won an Obie Award in 1964. Since 1980 he has taught at the State University of New York at Stony Brook, where he is professor emeritus.

DONALD JUSTICE (1925–2004), a poet and painter, received the Lamont Poetry Prize for his first volume, *The Summer Anniversaries* (1960), the Pulitzer Prize for *Selected Poems* (1979), and in 1991 the Bollingen Prize. A professor at the University of Iowa, Syracuse University, Princeton University, and the University of Florida–Gainesville, Justice taught many poets who would go on to become well known in their own right.

MARY KARR (b. 1955) was raised in East Texas, an experience she recounts in her 1995 memoir *The Liars' Club.* She is the author of three books of poems, including *The Devil's Tour* (1993) and *Viper Rum* (1998). Karr is professor of English at Syracuse University.

LAURA KASISCHKE (b. 1961) is the author of several novels and books of poetry, including *Lilies Without* (2007) and *Space, in Chains* (2011). Her novel *The Life before Her Eyes* was made into a film by Vadim Perelman, starring Uma Thurman and Evan Rachel Wood. She has received the Juniper Prize, the Alice Fay di Castagnola Award from the Poetry Society of America, and the Beatrice Hawley Award. Kasischke teaches at the University of Michigan.

WELDON KEES (1914–1955), author of the poetry collections *The Last Man* (1943) and *The Fall of Magicians* (1947), was also well known as a painter, art critic, and experimental filmmaker. In 1955 Kees took his sleeping bag and his savings account book and disappeared, leaving his car on the Golden Gate Bridge. He had told a friend he wanted to start a new life in Mexico, like Ambrose Bierce, but it is presumed he leapt from the bridge.

AUGUST KLEINZAHLER (b. 1949) studied at the University of Victoria under the English Modernist Basil Bunting. His many books include *Red Sauce, Whiskey and Snow* (1995), *Green Sees Things in Waves* (1999), and *The Strange Hours Travelers Keep* (2004), winner of the International Griffin Poetry Prize. Kleinzahler's volume of new and selected poems, *Sleeping It Off in Rapid City* (2008), was awarded the National Book Critics Circle Award. He published a memoir, *Cutty, One Rock*, in 2004.

MAXINE KUMIN (b. 1925) is author of many books including *House, Bridge, Fountain, Gate* (1975); *Our Ground Time Here Will Be Brief* (1982); *Looking for Luck* (1992), which received the Poets' Prize; *Bringing Together* (2003); *Still to Mow* (2009); and *Where I Live: New & Selected Poems 1990–2010. Up Country: Poems of New England* (1972) received the Pulitzer Prize. Kumin has received the Aiken Taylor Award for Modern Poetry, an American Academy of Arts and Letters award, the Sarah Joseph Hale Award, the Levinson Prize, and the Eunice Tietjens Memorial Prize from *Poetry*. She lives in New Hampshire.

DENISE LEVERTOV (1923–1997) was born in Ilford, England, a suburb of London. She and her older sister, Olga, were educated by their Welsh mother until the age of thirteen. Her first book of poems, *The Double Image*, was published in 1946. Levertov came to the United States in 1948. *Here and Now* appeared in 1957. Subsequent books include *With Eyes at the Back of Our Heads* (1959), *O Taste and SEE* (1964), *The Sorrow Dance* (1967), *The Freeing of the Dust* (1975), *Candles in Babylon* (1982), and *Evening Train* (1992). She received many awards, including the Shelley Memorial Award, the Robert Frost Medal, the Lenore Marshall Prize, and the Lannan Award. Levertov taught at several universities, including Brandeis, Massachusetts Institute of Technology, Tufts, and Stanford.

RODDY LUMSDEN (b. 1966) was born in St. Andrews, Scotland. His poetry collections include *Yeah, Yeah, Yeah* (1997), *Roddy Lumsden Is Dead* (2003), *Third Wish Wasted* (2009), and *Terrific Melancholy* (2011). The recipient of an Eric Gregory Award, Lumsden has worked as an editor, teacher, and writer of puzzles and quizzes for newspapers.

WILLIAM MATTHEWS (1942–1997) was the author of several books of poems, including *Ruining the New Road* (1970), *Rising and Falling* (1979), *Flood* (1982), *A Happy Childhood* (1984), and *Time and Money* (1995), which won the National Book Critics Circle Award. In 1997 he received the Ruth Lilly Poetry Prize. At the time of his death he was director of the creative writing program at the City College of New York.

SAMUEL MENASHE (1925–2011) grew up in Elmhurst, Queens, and studied at the Sorbonne. He published his first book, *No Jerusalem but This*, in 1961. He wrote several more books, including *The Niche Narrows* (2000), before receiving *Poetry*'s first Neglected Masters Award in 2004. A book of selected poems, edited by Christopher Ricks, followed in 2005 on the occasion of the poet's eightieth birthday. A revised edition, with ten additional poems, was published in 2008.

WILLIAM MEREDITH (1919–2007) served as the poet laureate consultant in poetry to the Library of Congress from 1978 to 1980. In 1944 his first collection, *Love Letter from an Impossible Land*, was chosen by Archibald MacLeish for publication in the Yale Series of Younger Poets. Meredith received both the Pulitzer Prize and a *Los Angeles Times* Book Award for *Partial Accounts: New and Selected Poems* (1987) and the National Book Award for *Effort at Speech: New and Selected Poems* (1997).

JAMES MERRILL (1926–1995) was the son of investment banker Charles E. Merrill, cofounder of the Merrill Lynch brokerage firm. His first book, *The Black Swan*, was published in 1946. Merrill received two National Book Awards, for *Nights and Days* (1966) and *Mirabell: Books of Numbers* (1978). His Ouija-inspired epic poem *The Changing Light at Sandover* (1982) won the National Book Critics Circle Award, and he was awarded the inaugural Bobbitt National Prize for Poetry by the Library of Congress for *The Inner Room* (1988); he also received both the Bollingen Prize in Poetry and the Pulitzer Prize, the latter for *Divine Comedies* (1976).

W. S. MERWIN (b. 1927) was born the son of a Presbyterian minister. W. H. Auden chose his first book, *The Mask of Janus*, for the Yale Younger Poets Series in 1952. *The Lice* was published in 1967 and remains his most well-known work. *The Carrier of Ladders* (1970) won the Pulitzer Prize, which Merwin won again for *The Shadow of Sirius* (2008). Other books include *The Moving Target* (1963), *The Compass Flower* (1977), *The Rain in the Trees* (1988), and *The Vixen* (1996). Merwin has been the recipient of the Bollingen Prize, the Aiken Taylor Award for Modern American Poetry, the Ruth Lilly Poetry Prize, the PEN Translation Prize, the Shelley Memorial Award, the Wallace Stevens Award, and a Lila Wallace-*Reader's Digest* Writers' Award. He served as US poet laureate from 2010 to 2011.

JOSEPHINE MILES (1911–1985) spent her entire academic career at the University of California, Berkeley, where she was the first woman to be tenured in the English Department. She published over a dozen books of poetry, including *Lines at Intersection* (1939), *Kinds of Affection* (1967), and *To All Appearances* (1974). Her *Collected Poems* (1983) received the Lenore Marshall Poetry Prize and was a finalist for the Pulitzer Prize. Miles also published several scholarly works on poetic language and style.

EDNA ST. VINCENT MILLAY (1892–1950) was brought to public notice in 1912, when her poem "Renascence" received fourth place in a poetry contest. *Renascence, and Other Poems* was published in 1917. *A Few Figs from Thistles* followed in 1920, and *The Ballad of the Harp-Weaver* won the Pulitzer Prize in 1923. Millay was also known for her social activism; in 1927 she was arrested while protesting the execution of the Italian anarchists Sacco and Vanzetti. She was awarded the Frost Medal in 1943.

ANGE MLINKO (b. 1969) is the author of three books of poetry, including *Starred Wire* (2005), a National Poetry Series winner, and *Shoulder Season* (2010). In 2009 she won the Poetry Foundation's Randall Jarrell Award in Criticism. Mlinko is currently assistant professor in the University of Houston creative writing program.

MARIANNE MOORE (1887–1972) graduated from Bryn Mawr College in 1909 and began to publish poems in 1915. In 1925 Moore became editor of *The Dial,* a post she held until the magazine ceased publication in 1929. From that point onward, Moore made her living writing poetry and reviews. Her books include *What Are Years* (1941), *Like a Bulwark* (1956), and *O to Be a Dragon* (1961). *Collected Poems* (1951) received the National Book Award in 1952, the Pulitzer Prize in 1952, and the Bollingen Prize in 1953.

LISEL MUELLER (b. 1924) has had a career both writing poetry and translating. Her collections of poetry include *The Private Life*, which was the 1975 Lamont Poetry Selection; *Second Language* (1986); *The Need to Hold Still* (1980), winner of the National Book Award; *Learning to Play by Ear* (1990); and *Alive Together: New & Selected Poems* (1996), which won the Pulitzer Prize.

Her other awards and honors include the Ruth Lilly Poetry Prize and a fellowship from the National Endowment for the Arts.

LORINE NIEDECKER (1903–1970) was born in Fort Atkinson, Wisconsin, and lived in this wilderness area for most of her life. Niedecker chose to write in seclusion, and many of her closest relatives and neighbors were unaware that she was a poet. Although her long correspondence with Cid Corman, who frequently published her poems in his journal, *Origin*, brought her some critical notice, her work was generally overlooked until late in her life. Her first book, *New Goose* (1946), was privately printed, and her second, *My Friend Tree*, which did not appear until 1962, was published in England. Niedecker attracted significant critical attention only with *North Central* (1968). Her *Collected Works* was published in 2002.

FRANK O'HARA (1926–1966)—along with John Ashbery, Kenneth Koch, and James Schuyler—was a key member of a group known, jokily, as the New York School of poets. A friend of several prominent New York artists, including Willem de Kooning and Larry Rivers, he was assistant curator of painting and sculpture exhibitions for the Museum of Modern Art. His books include *Meditations in an Emergency* (1956) and *Lunch Poems* (1964). His *Collected Poems* (1971) won the National Book Award. O'Hara died after being hit by a dune buggy on Fire Island.

GEORGE OPPEN (1908–1984) was best known as a poet of the Objectivist school. After the publication of his first book, *Discrete Series*, in 1934, he abandoned poetry to concentrate on political activism, moving to Mexico to avoid the attentions of the House Un-American Activities Committee. He returned to the United States and to poetry in 1958. *Of Being Numerous* won the Pulitzer Prize in 1969. Oppen's other books are *The Materials* (1962), *This in Which* (1965), *Seascape: Needle's Eye* (1972), and *Collected Poems* (1975). His *New Collected Poems* was published in 2001.

P. K. PAGE (1916–2010) was born in England and moved to Alberta, Canada, at the age of four. She was the author of ten books of poetry, including *Planet Earth* (2002), *Cosmologies* (2003), and *Coal and Roses* (2009). A novelist and short-story writer, Page also wrote an autobiography and several works for children and painted under the name P. K. Irwin. She received the Terasen Lifetime Achievement Award and the Lieutenant Governor's Award for Literary Excellence. In 2007 Page was named a Fellow of the Royal Society of Canada.

DON PATERSON (b. 1963) was born in Dundee, Scotland. He left school at sixteen and moved to London to pursue music and join a band. Paterson's first poetry collection, *Nil Nil* (1993), won the Forward Prize for Best First Collection. *God's Gift to Women* (1997) won both the T. S. Eliot Prize and the Geoffrey Faber Memorial Prize, and *Landing Light* (2003) won the Whitbread Poetry Award and an unprecedented second T. S. Eliot Prize. *Rain* (2009) also won the Forward Prize. In 2008, for his service to literature, Paterson was appointed Officer of the Order of the British Empire.

SYLVIA PLATH (1932–1963) began writing poetry at the age of eight and had already published work in several magazines by the time she arrived at Smith College in 1950. *The Colossus and Other Poems* appeared in 1960; the semiautobiographical novel *The Bell Jar* was published in 1963. Plath's fame rests chiefly on her final poems, collected under the title *Ariel* and published after her suicide by her husband, Ted Hughes. In 1982 she became the first poet to be posthumously awarded the Pulitzer Prize, for *The Collected Poems*.

MARIE PONSOT (b. 1921) published her first book, *True Minds*, in Lawrence Ferlinghetti's City Lights series in 1956. She did not publish another volume until 1981, focusing instead on her career as a translator. *The Bird Catcher* (1998) received the National Book Critics Circle Award. She teaches in the graduate writing program at Columbia University in New York City.

EZRA POUND (1885–1972) is best known for his innovations in literature, from *Cathay*'s versions of Chinese poetry (1915) to the monument of *The Cantos*. But he was also Modernism's greatest champion, working to advance the fortunes of T. S. Eliot, James Joyce, Robert Frost, and others, leading Eliot to claim that Pound "is more responsible for the twentieth-century revolution in poetry than is any other individual." After he made a series of broadcasts on Italian radio critical of the Allied war effort, Pound was arrested by American forces in 1945. Declared unfit to stand trial for treason, he was confined to St. Elizabeths psychiatric hospital in Washington, DC, where he would remain for twelve years. He was awarded the first Bollingen Prize in 1949, amid much controversy, for *The Pisan Cantos*.

BELLE RANDALL (b. 1940) is the poetry editor of *Common Knowledge* and the author of *The Coast Starlight* (2010). Her work first appeared in *Poetry* in 1961.

ADRIENNE RICH (1929–2012) won the Yale Younger Poets Award in 1951 for *A Change of World*. Subsequent books include *Necessities of Life* (1966), *Leaflets* (1969), *The Will to Change* (1971), *Time's Power: Poems, 1985–1988* (1988), *An Atlas of the Difficult World: Poems, 1988–1991* (1991), and *Dark Fields of the Republic, 1991–1995* (1995). *Diving into the Wreck: Poems 1971–1972* (1973) won the National Book Award. *The School among the Ruins: Poems, 2000–2004* (2004) received the National Book Critics Circle Award. Rich was also the recipient of the Ruth

Lilly Poetry Prize, the Lannan Lifetime Achievement Award, the Bollingen Prize, and the Academy of American Poets Fellowship. She taught at several universities, including Brandeis, Rutgers, Cornell, and Stanford.

ATSURO RILEY (b. 1960) grew up in South Carolina. He is the author of *Romey's Order* (2010), which won the Kate Tufts Discovery Award, *The Believer* Poetry Award, and a Witter Bynner Award from the Library of Congress. Riley received the J. Howard and M. J. Wood Prize from *Poetry* magazine. He lives in California.

EDWIN ARLINGTON ROBINSON's (1869–1935) poetic vision, as expressed in such character-driven poems as "Richard Cory" and "Aaron Stark," was influenced by a number of early tragedies. His books include *The Torrent and the Night Before* (1896) and *The Children of the Night*, originally published in 1897 and reissued by Scribner's in 1905 at Theodore Roosevelt's behest.

THEODORE ROETHKE (1908–1963) briefly attended law school at the University of Michigan before dedicating himself to poetry. His first book, *Open Houses*, appeared in 1941; subsequent volumes include *The Lost Son* (1948), *Praise to the End!* (1951), *Words for the Wind* (1957), and *The Far Field*, awarded the National Book Award in 1965. Roethke also wrote several poems for children. Plagued by breakdowns, he spent his later life in and out of sanitariums, but was a dedicated teacher. His students included David Wagoner, and, at the University of Washington, James Wright and Richard Hugo.

ISAAC ROSENBERG (1890–1918), born in Bristol to Jewish immigrants from Russia, fought in World War I from 1915 to 1918. He published only two privately printed books in his lifetime, *Night and Day* (1912) and *Youth* (1915). *Poems*, published in 1922, contained the war poems for which he is best remembered. Rosenberg was killed at the age of twenty-eight in the battle of Arras.

MURIEL RUKEYSER (1913–1980) was well known for her poetic interest in feminism, social activism, and Judaism. In 1935 her collection *Theory of Flight* was chosen for publication in the Yale Younger Poets Series. *The Book of the Dead* (1938) remembers the miners who died in the Hawks Nest Tunnel disaster in West Virginia. Other books include *A Turning Wind* (1939), *Beast in View* (1944), *Body of Waking* (1958), and *Waterlily Fire* (1962). In the sixties and seventies Rukeyser's work was popular among feminists and the antiwar movement.

KAY RYAN (b. 1945) is the author of several books of poetry, including *Flamingo Watching* (2006), *The Niagara River* (2005), and *Say Uncle* (2000). *The*

Best of It: New and Selected Poems (2010) won the Pulitzer Prize for Poetry. Ryan served as US poet laureate from 2008 to 2010.

JACOB SAENZ (b. 1982) earned a BA in creative writing from Columbia College in Chicago and won a Letras Latinas Residency Fellowship at the Anderson Center in Red Wing, Minnesota. Saenz has been an editor at *Columbia Poetry Review* and an associate editor at *RHINO*. He works as an acquisitions assistant at the Columbia College library.

JAMES SCHUYLER (1923–1991) was, with John Ashbery, Frank O'Hara, and Kenneth Koch, a leading member of the New York School of poets. In 1947 Schuyler moved to Italy to serve as W. H. Auden's secretary. From 1955 to 1961, he was a curator of circulating exhibitions at the Museum of Modern Art. He also wrote art criticism for *Art News*. His first major collection, *Freely Espousing* (1969), won the Frank O'Hara Prize. Other books include *The Crystal Lithium* (1972), *Hymn to Life* (1974), and *The Morning of the Poem* (1980), for which he received the Pulitzer Prize. Schuyler was also the coauthor, with John Ashbery, of a novel, *A Nest of Ninnies* (1969). His *Collected Poems* were published in 1993.

DELMORE SCHWARTZ (1913–1966), a poet, playwright, and short-story writer from Brooklyn, New York, published *In Dreams Begin Responsibilities*, a collection of stories and poems, in 1938. In 1959 he was awarded the Bollingen Prize for *Summer Knowledge: New and Selected Poems*, becoming the youngest-ever recipient of that honor. His life was frequently disordered by mental illness; when he died, his body lay unclaimed for three days.

FREDERICK SEIDEL (b. 1936) was born the son of a coal magnate. His first book, *Final Solutions* (1963), was chosen by Robert Lowell, Louise Bogan, and Stanley Kunitz for a prize offered by the 92nd Street Y. The manuscript was rejected by the committee and publisher for what they saw as its anti-Catholic, anti-Semitic, and libelous tone. Lowell, Bogan, and Kunitz resigned from the board in protest, and the book was published the following year. Seidel has published over a dozen collections of poetry since, including the National Book Critics Circle Award–winning *Sunrise* (1979), Pulitzer Prize nominee *Going Fast* (1998), and *Ooga-Booga* (2006). Seidel's collected poems were published in 2009 as *Poems 1959–2009*.

GARY SNYDER (b. 1930), often associated with the Beats and with the San Francisco Renaissance, published *Riprap* in 1959. His several subsequent books include *Myths and Texts* (1960), *The Back Country* (1967), *Turtle Island* (1974), *Axe Handles* (1983), *No Nature: New and Selected Poems* (1992), and

Mountains and Rivers without End (1996). Snyder is also the author of several books on ecology. He has received the Bollingen Prize, an American Academy of Arts and Letters award, the Bess Hokin Prize and the Levinson Prize from *Poetry*, the Robert Kirsch Lifetime Achievement Award from the *Los Angeles Times*, the Shelley Memorial Award, and the Ruth Lilly Poetry Prize. Snyder is professor of English at the University of California–Davis.

JACK SPICER (1925–1965) was born in Los Angeles to midwestern parents and raised in a Calvinist home. While attending the University of California–Berkeley, Spicer met fellow poets Robin Blaser and Robert Duncan. The three would spearhead what became known as the San Francisco Renaissance. At Berkeley Spicer studied linguistics but lost his teaching assistantship after refusing to sign a loyalty oath. He spent most of his life in San Francisco working as a researcher in linguistics. His books include *After Lorca* (1957), *The Holy Grail* (1964), *Language* (1965), and *Book of Magazine Verse* (1966). *My Vocabulary Did This to Me: The Collected Poetry of Jack Spicer* (2009) won the American Book Award for poetry.

A. E. STALLINGS (b. 1968) studied classics in Athens, Georgia, and has lived since 1999 in Athens, Greece. She has published two books of poetry, *Archaic Smile* (1999), which won the Richard Wilbur Award, and *Hapax* (2000). Her translation of Lucretius's *The Nature of Things* was published in 2007. In 2011 she received a MacArthur Foundation Fellowship.

GEORGE STARBUCK (1931–1996) enrolled at the California Institute of Technology to study mathematics at age sixteen but dropped out after two years to focus on poetry. His first book of poems, *Bone Thoughts*, won the Yale Series of Younger Poets competition in 1960. Starbuck taught at the Iowa Writers Workshop, Boston University, and the State University of New York at Buffalo. He received the Lenore Marshall Poetry Prize in 1982 for *The Argot Merchant Disaster: Poems, New and Selected*.

WALLACE STEVENS (1879–1955) worked briefly as a journalist before attending the New York School of Law. In 1916 he joined the Hartford Accident and Indemnity Company, where he remained employed for the rest of his life, becoming vice president in 1934. Stevens was also one of the preeminent poets of American Modernism, although his first book, *Harmonium*, was generally ignored upon its publication in 1923. Subsequent volumes include *Ideas of Order* (1936), *Parts of a World* (1952), and *Transport to Summer* (1957). Stevens was awarded the National Book Award in 1951 for *The Auroras of Autumn* and again in 1955 for his *Collected Poems*, which also earned him the Pulitzer Prize. In 1950 he became the recipient of the second Bollingen Prize.

ANNE STEVENSON (b. 1933) was born in Cambridge, England, and moved between the United Kingdom and the United States several times during the first half of her life. In 2007 Stevenson was awarded the Lannan Lifetime Achievement Award for Poetry and the Poetry Foundation's Neglected Masters Award. She has also received the Northern Rock Foundation Writer's Award. She is the author of several books of poetry and prose, including *Living in America* (1965), *Reversals* (1969), *Enough of Green* (1977), *Minute by Glass Minute* (1972), *A Report from the Border* (2003), and *Bitter Fame* (1989), a biography of Sylvia Plath.

RUTH STONE (1915–2011) published her first book of poems, *In an Iridescent Time*, in 1958. She won the National Book Critics Circle Award for *Ordinary Words* (1999) and the National Book Award for *In the Next Galaxy* (2002). *What Love Comes To: New and Selected Poems* (2008) was a finalist for the Pulitzer Prize. She was professor of English and creative writing at the State University of New York at Binghamton.

MAY SWENSON (1913–1989) was born into a Mormon household in Logan, Utah. Her books include *Another Animal* (1954), *To Mix with Time: New and Selected Poems* (1963), *Half Sun, Half Sleep* (1967), *Iconographs* (1970), and *In Other Words* (1987). Swenson received several awards throughout her career including the William Rose Benet Prize of the Poetry Society of America in 1959, the National Institute of Arts and Letters Award in 1960, the Shelley Poetry Award in 1968, and the Bollingen Prize in 1981.

JEANNE MURRAY WALKER (b. 1944) is the author of seven books of poetry, including *Coming into History* (1991), *A Deed to the Light* (2004), and *New Tracks, Night Falling* (2009). She is a professor at the University of Delaware. Walker's new and selected poems will be published in 2012.

RACHEL WETZSTEON (1967–2009) published three collections of poetry: National Poetry Series winner *The Other Stars* (1994), *Home and Away* (1998), and *Sakura Park* (2006), as well as *Influential Ghosts* (2007), a critical study of W. H. Auden. Wetzsteon received the American Academy of Arts and Letters' Witter Bynner Prize for Poetry. She taught at the 92nd Street Y's Unterberg Poetry Center in New York and William Patterson University in New Jersey and at the time of her death had recently joined *The New Republic* as their poetry editor.

RICHARD WILBUR (b. 1921) won the Pulitzer Prize and National Book Award for his collection *Things of This World* in 1957 and a second Pulitzer for *New and Collected Poems*. He has won the Wallace Stevens Award, the Frost Medal, the Aiken Taylor Award for Modern American Poetry, two Bollingen Prizes, the T. S. Eliot Award, the Edna St. Vincent Millay Memorial Award, and the Ruth Lilly Prize. Wilbur taught for twenty years at Wesleyan University and served as U.S. poet laureate from 1987 to 1988.

WILLIAM CARLOS WILLIAMS (1883–1963) received his MD from the University of Pennsylvania, where he befriended Ezra Pound. He later said that "before meeting Pound is like B.C. and A.D." Williams was invited to become poetry consultant to the Library of Congress in 1949 but delayed acceptance because of poor health until 1952. The invitation was withdrawn after accusations of Williams's communist affiliations were circulated. His major works include *Kora in Hell* (1920), *Spring and All* (1923), *Pictures from Brueghel and Other Poems* (1962), the five-volume epic *Paterson* (1963), and *Imaginations* (1970). He also wrote several works of prose, most notably *In the American Grain* (1925).

ELEANOR WILNER's (b. 1937) books of poems include *Otherwise* (1993) and *Reversing the Spell* (1998). She is also the author of the critical study *Gathering the Winds: Visionary Imagination and Radical Transformation of Self and Society* (1975). Wilner served as editor of *American Poetry Review* and has taught at the University of Chicago, Northwestern University, and Smith College.

CHARLES WRIGHT (b. 1935) is the author of several collections of poetry, including *The World of the Ten Thousand Things* (1990), *Chickamauga* (1995), and *Scar Tissue* (2006), which was awarded the Griffin International Poetry Prize. *Black Zodiac* (1997) received both the Pulitzer Prize and the National Book Critics Circle Award. Recipient as well of the 1993 Ruth Lilly Poetry Prize, Wright is professor of English at the University of Virginia.

JAMES WRIGHT (1927–1980) studied at the University of Washington with Theodore Roethke and received the Yale Younger Poets Prize in 1956 for *The Green Wall*. Subsequent books include *The Branch Will Not Break* (1963), *Shall We Gather at the River* (1967), *Two Citizens* (1973), and *To a Blossoming Pear Tree* (1977). *Collected Poems* (1971) won the Pulitzer Prize. *Above the River: Complete Poems* was published in 1992. He taught at the University of Minnesota and Hunter College.

WILLIAM BUTLER YEATS (1865–1939) was born in Dublin, Ireland. A member of the Protestant, Anglo-Irish minority, he became involved early in occultism and Irish nationalism, although the latter interest was tempered by the time he accepted a six-year appointment to the senate of the Irish Free State in December 1922. From the early poems of *The Wind among the Reeds* (1899) and *In the Seven Woods* (1903) to the late monuments of *The Tower* (1928) and *New Poems* (1938), Yeats was one of the greatest poets of the twentieth century. He was awarded the Nobel Prize for Literature in 1923.